Chakras: Chakra Healing for Beginners

Maya Whitaker

Published by CiJiRO Publishing, 2023.

CHAKRAS: CHAKRA HEALING FOR BEGINNERS

First edition. June 30, 2023.

Copyright © 2023 Maya Whitaker.

ISBN: 979-8223084174

Written by Maya Whitaker.

Table of Contents

Chapter 1: Exploring the Basics: Understanding Chakras and Energy Centers

Are you interested in understanding the mysterious power of chakras and energy centers? You've come to the right place! In this chapter, we will explore the fundamentals of chakras and energy centers. We will start by looking at the basics of chakras and energy centers, and then delve deeper into their properties and how to tap into them. By the end, you will have a thorough understanding of these powerful forces and how to use them in your daily life. So, let's get started on our journey into the world of chakras and energy centers!

What are Chakras and Energy Centers?

Chakras and energy centers are a fundamental part of our being, affecting everything from our physical health to our emotional and spiritual well-being. At their core, chakras are spinning wheels of energy located throughout our bodies. These energy centers work together to keep our body and mind in harmony and balance.

The word "chakra" comes from the Sanskrit language and means "wheel." This term was first introduced in the ancient Indian spiritual texts known as the Upanishads, which date back to around 600 BCE. The concept of chakras is closely associated with Hindu and Buddhist spiritual practices, but it is also relevant in other spiritual traditions, such as Taoism and Reiki.

The chakra system includes seven primary energy centers that are located along the spine. Each of these centers corresponds to a specific area of the body and is associated with specific emotions and functions.

The seven chakras are:

- Root Chakra

- Sacral Chakra

- Solar Plexus Chakra

- Heart Chakra

- Throat Chakra

- Third Eye Chakra

- Crown Chakra

It is said that these chakras each represent a particular color, symbol, and vibration. When our chakras are balanced and harmonious, we experience physical health, emotional stability, and spiritual fulfillment. However, when our chakras are blocked or out of balance, we may experience physical or emotional symptoms.

Understanding chakras and energy centers is essential to maintaining optimal health and well-being. By learning more about the chakra system, we can begin to work with our energy centers to create a healthier, more balanced life.

History and Origins of the Chakra System

In ancient Indian texts like the Vedas and Upanishads, chakras are discussed. The word "chakra" comes from the Sanskrit word meaning "wheel" or "circle," and the chakra system is believed to be an energy map of the human body.

The earliest references to chakras can be found in the Upanishads, which are a collection of texts that date back to 500 BCE. In these texts, chakras are described as centers of spiritual power that are located along the spinal cord.

Over time, the chakra system evolved and became an important part of the Hindu and Buddhist traditions. In Hinduism, chakras are seen as energy centers that can be activated through yoga, meditation, and other spiritual practices. In Buddhism, the chakra system is used to understand the nature of the mind and achieve enlightenment.

The chakra system was introduced to the West in the early 20th century by Sir John Woodroffe, a British judge who wrote extensively about Tantra and Hindu philosophy. Woodroffe's books on the subject helped popularize the concept of chakras in the West, and today, the chakra system is widely studied and practiced by people around the world.

While the history and origins of the chakra system may be complex and multifaceted, what is clear is that it has stood the test of time as a powerful tool for spiritual growth and well-being. By understanding the fundamentals of chakras and energy centers, we can tap into their transformative power and unlock our full potential as human beings.

The chakra system is based on the belief that the human body is made up of energy, and that this energy can be channeled and balanced through the chakras. There are seven main chakras in the body, each associated with a different color, symbol, and aspect of life.

The root chakra is located at the base of the spine and is associated with grounding and survival. Belonging to the lower abdomen, the sacral chakra is associated with creativity and sexuality. The solar plexus chakra, located in the upper abdomen, is associated with personal power and self-confidence. The heart chakra, located in the center of the chest, is associated with love and compassion. The throat chakra, located at the base of the neck, is associated with communication and self-expression. The third eye chakra, located between the eyebrows, is associated with intuition and spiritual insight. Spirituality and connection to the divine are associated with the crown chakra. When these chakras are balanced and harmonious, we experience a sense of physical, emotional, and spiritual well-being. However, when one or more of the chakras are blocked or imbalanced, we may experience physical ailments, emotional issues, and spiritual disconnect.

By learning how to activate and balance our chakras, we can promote healing and growth in all areas of our lives. Through yoga, meditation, energy healing, and other practices, we can tap into the transformative power of the chakra system and unlock our full potential as human beings.

Structure and Characteristics of the Chakra System

The Chakra System is composed of seven energy centers that are aligned along the spinal column. These centers represent different aspects of our physical, emotional, and spiritual well-being and are linked to specific body organs, emotions, and life areas. Color, sound, and vibration frequency are associated with each chakra.Starting from the bottom, the Root Chakra (Muladhara) is located at the base of the spine and is associated with grounding, safety, and survival instincts. The Sacral Chakra (Svadhisthana) is located just below the navel and is associated with sexuality, creativity, and passion.

The Solar Plexus Chakra (Manipura) is located in the upper abdomen and is associated with personal power, confidence, and self-esteem. The Heart Chakra (Anahata) is located in the center of the chest and is associated with love, compassion, and forgiveness.

The Throat Chakra (Vishuddha) is located in the throat and is associated with communication, self-expression, and authenticity. The Third Eye Chakra (Ajna) is located in the center of the forehead and is associated with intuition, wisdom, and clarity of thought.

The Crown Chakra (Sahasrara) is located at the top of the head and is associated with spirituality, higher consciousness, and divine connection.

The Chakra System is often depicted as a spinning wheel or vortex of energy that rotate

s clockwise, drawing in energy from the universe and distributing it throughout the body.

When a chakra is blocked or imbalanced, it can lead to physical, emotional, and spiritual disturbances. It is important to maintain balanced and harmonious chakras to promote overall health and well-being. In the next chapter, we will dive deeper into the relationship between chakras and physical, emotional, and spiritual well-being.

The Chakra System is often depicted as a spinning wheel or vortex of energy that rotates clockwise, drawing in energy from the universe and distributing it throughout the body. When a chakra is blocked or imbalanced, it can lead to physical, emotional, and spiritual disturbances. It is important to maintain balanced and harmonious chakras to promote overall health and well-being. There are various ways to balance the chakras, including yoga, meditation, energy healing, sound therapy, and aromatherapy.

By working with the chakras, we can gain a deeper understanding of ourselves and the interconnectedness of all things. Understanding the basics of chakras and energy centers is an essential first step in our journey towards greater self-awareness and spiritual growth. In the next chapter, we will explore the relationship between chakras and physical, emotional, and spiritual well-being, and discuss the signs of imbalanced chakras to look out for.

The Relationship between Chakras and Physical, Emotional, and Spiritual Well-being

The chakra system is intimately linked with our physical, emotional, and spiritual well-being. Each chakra is associated with specific organs, glands, and body functions, and blockages or imbalances in these energy centers can lead to physical and emotional problems.

For example, the root chakra, located at the base of the spine, is associated with our sense of security, stability, and survival. If this chakra is blocked or imbalanced, we may experience physical symptoms such as constipation, lower back pain, or issues with our legs and feet. Emotionally, we may feel anxious or fearful about our place in the world or have difficulty trusting others.

Similarly, the sacral chakra, located in the lower abdomen, is associated with our creativity, sexuality, and emotional balance. An imbalance in this chakra may manifest as reproductive issues, digestive problems, or difficulties with our emotions and relationships.

By understanding the relationship between our chakras and our physical, emotional, and spiritual well-being, we can begin to identify and address any imbalances or blockages that may be impacting our health and happiness. Through practices such as yoga, meditation, and energy healing, we can work to restore balance and harmony to our chakra system, supporting our overall well-being and vitality.

The heart chakra, located in the center of the chest, is associated with love, compassion, and emotional healing. When this chakra is balanced, we feel a deep sense of connection to others and experience positive relationships. However, an imbalance in this chakra can lead to issues such as heart disease, asthma, or emotional detachment.

The throat chakra, which is located in the neck, is linked to communication and self-expression. An imbalance in this chakra may result in problems such as thyroid disorders, voice issues, or difficulty expressing ourselves authentically.

The third eye chakra, located in the forehead, is associated with intuition and spiritual connection. Imbalances in this chakra may result in headaches, vision problems, or difficulties with insight and clarity.

Finally, the crown chakra, located at the top of the head, is associated with spiritual awareness and connection to the divine. When this chakra is balanced, we feel a sense of purpose and alignment with our higher self. However, imbalances in this chakra can result in issues such as depression, neurological disorders, or feelings of disconnection and emptiness.

By understanding the connection between our chakras and our overall well-being, we can take steps to support our physical, emotional, and spiritual health. This may involve practices such as yoga, meditation, or energy healing, as well as incorporating healthy habits into our daily routine, such as regular exercise, a balanced diet, and adequate sleep. Ultimately, when our chakras are balanced and harmonious, we experience greater health, happiness, and fulfillment in our lives.

The Importance of Maintaining Balanced and Harmonious Chakras

Just like how we need to maintain our physical health by eating well and exercising regularly, we also need to maintain our energetic health by keeping our chakras balanced and harmonious. When our chakras are out of balance, we may experience physical symptoms like headaches, fatigue, and digestive issues. We may also feel emotionally unstable or experience mental fog.

By understanding the chakra system and learning how to balance and harmonize our chakras, we can experience greater physical, emotional, and spiritual well-being. Balanced chakras help us feel more energized, focused, and confident in our daily lives. They can also support our spiritual growth by helping us connect to our inner selves and higher consciousness.

There are many practices and techniques for balancing and harmonizing the chakras, including meditation, yoga, reiki, and other energy-healing modalities. It is essential to find a practice that resonates with you and fits your lifestyle.

Maintaining balanced and harmonious chakras is an ongoing practice that requires regular attention and self-reflection. It is not something that can be achieved overnight, but with dedication and mindfulness, we can cultivate a healthy and vibrant energy system that supports our overall well-being.

It's also important to note that balancing our chakras isn't a one-time fix. Our energy centers are constantly affected by our thoughts, emotions, and external factors, so it's crucial to continuously check in with ourselves and our chakras to ensure that we're maintaining balance and harmony.

Additionally, different chakras may require more attention at different times depending on what we're experiencing in our lives. For example, if we're going through a period of stress or anxiety, we may need to focus more on balancing our root and sacral chakras to feel more grounded and stable.

Overall, understanding and working with the chakra system can be a transformative and empowering journey. By learning about our energy centers and how to keep them in balance, we can cultivate greater awareness, vitality, and connection to ourselves and the world around us.

Chapter 2: The Root Chakra: Grounding and Stability

Exploring the Root Chakra: Finding Your Grounding and Stability

Are you feeling a little dizzy? Do you feel disconnected from your surroundings and disconnected from your body? This chapter is about the first of the seven major energy centers in the body: the root chakra. The root chakra brings stability, balance, and connection into our lives. Here are some topics we'll talk about how to identify the root chakra, its links to physical and emotional symptoms, and ways to open and balance it for increased well-being.

Understanding the Root Chakra

Located at the base of the spine, the root chakra is also called Muladhara. This chakra is responsible for our sense of grounding and stability, which are fundamental for our emotional and physical well-being.

The root chakra is associated with the earth element and the color red, symbolizing stability, strength, and security. It is responsible for our sense of safety, survival, and our connection to the physical world.

A balanced root chakra helps us feel grounded, safe, and secure in our environment, allowing us to focus on other areas of our life without worry or fear. However, an imbalanced root chakra can result in feelings of anxiety, fear, insecurity, and even physical ailments such as lower back pain, immune system issues, or digestive problems.

Understanding the root chakra is essential to cultivating balance and harmony within ourselves and our environment. By acknowledging its importance and learning to balance it, we can create a strong foundation for our well-being.

To balance the root chakra, we need to identify any signs of imbalance and work towards cultivating a sense of grounding and stability. This can be achieved through various techniques, such as yoga, meditation, breathing exercises, and grounding activities.

When the root chakra is balanced, we feel connected to the present moment and our physical body, which allows us to move forward with confidence and a sense of security. A balanced root chakra also helps us to cultivate healthy relationships and strong connections with others.

However, when the root chakra is out of balance, we may experience feelings of anxiety, fear, or disconnection. This can manifest in various ways, such as difficulty sleeping, digestive problems, or even financial issues.

By focusing on strengthening our root chakra, we can cultivate a sense of grounding and stability that will allow us to navigate life with more ease and confidence. In the following sections, we'll explore some techniques and daily practices for balancing and strengthening the root chakra.

Characteristics of a Balanced Root Chakra

A balanced Root Chakra is associated with a sense of safety and security, both physically and emotionally. When the Root Chakra is in balance, you feel grounded and connected to the earth. This creates a strong foundation that allows you to move through life with stability and ease.

Balanced root chakras have the following characteristics:

1. Groundedness: You feel connected to the present moment and are able to anchor yourself in reality. You have a deep sense of being rooted and grounded.

2. Vitality: You have a strong physical energy that supports your health and well-being. You are able to maintain your body and mind in good condition.

3. Security: You feel a sense of security in the world. You are able to trust that you have what you need to survive and thrive.

4. Stability: You have a stable sense of self, which gives you the ability to navigate life's challenges with ease. You are confident in your own abilities and your place in the world.

5. Self-care: You prioritize taking care of yourself, both physically and emotionally. You are able to maintain a healthy balance between work and rest.

A balanced Root Chakra helps you to establish a solid foundation for your life, which makes it easier for you to manifest your goals and desires. When this chakra is balanced, you feel more confident and capable, which leads to greater success in all areas of your life.

Signs of an Imbalanced Root Chakra

An imbalanced Root Chakra can manifest in different ways. Here are some signs to look out for:

1. Feeling ungrounded: You might feel like you're disconnected from your body or the world around you. You may find it hard to concentrate or stay focused on tasks.

2. Fear and anxiety: When your Root Chakra is out of balance, you might feel anxious, fearful, or paranoid. You might also experience feelings of insecurity, self-doubt, and mistrust.

3. Physical issues: Since the Root Chakra is associated with the physical body, an imbalance in this area can cause various physical symptoms. These might include issues like lower back pain, digestive problems, and adrenal fatigue.

4. Financial difficulties: The Root Chakra is also associated with our ability to attract and manage financial resources. An imbalanced Root Chakra can make it hard to stay financially stable or secure.

5. Self-destructive behaviors: An imbalanced Root Chakra can also lead to negative self-talk, self-sabotage, and addictive behaviors.

If you're experiencing any of these symptoms, it's worth taking some time to focus on balancing your Root Chakra. By doing so, you can bring more stability and groundedness into your life.

The Importance of Grounding and Stability

Our energy system is based on the Muladhara, or root, chakra. It is located at the base of our spine and is associated with grounding and stability. When this chakra is balanced, we feel a sense of safety and security, both physically and emotionally.

Grounding is the process of connecting ourselves to the Earth's energy, allowing us to feel more centered and anchored. It helps us stay present and focused in the moment, while also promoting a sense of calmness and inner peace. Stability, on the other hand, refers to our ability to maintain a steady and consistent energy flow.

The root chakra governs our basic survival needs such as shelter, food, water, and safety. A balanced root chakra allows us to meet these needs without fear or worry. It also helps us establish a strong foundation for personal growth and development.

Contrastingly, an imbalanced root chakra may cause feelings of anxiety, insecurity, and restlessness. We may find it difficult to feel safe in our environment or trust our instincts. This can affect our physical health as well, causing issues with digestion, circulation, and immunity.

Therefore, it is important to prioritize grounding and stability in our daily lives. This can be achieved through practices such as meditation, yoga, and connecting with nature. By staying rooted in the present moment, we can create a sense of inner peace and harmony.

In addition, incorporating healthy habits such as a balanced diet, regular exercise, and consistent sleep patterns can also help balance the root chakra. When we take care of our physical body, we also support our emotional and energetic well-being.

In summary, the root chakra is an essential component of our energy system, governing our sense of grounding and stability. By prioritizing practices that promote these qualities, we can cultivate a sense of safety and security in our lives, allowing us to thrive and grow.

Techniques for Balancing the Root Chakra

Now that you have a better understanding of the Root Chakra and its significance, let's delve into some techniques that can help you balance it. Here are a few techniques to get started:

1. Yoga poses:

Certain yoga poses can be incredibly helpful for balancing the Root Chakra. Some of the most effective poses include Tree Pose, Warrior Pose, and Bridge Pose. These postures help connect the body to the ground, promote a sense of stability, and create a feeling of rootedness.

2. Meditation:

Meditation can also be an effective way to balance the Root Chakra. To begin, find a comfortable seated position, close your eyes, and focus on your breath. Imagine yourself as a tree with roots firmly planted in the ground. Visualize these roots growing deeper and deeper, grounding you even more. This simple visualization can be incredibly powerful in balancing your Root Chakra.

3. Crystal Healing:

Certain crystals are believed to help balance the Root Chakra. Red jasper, garnet, and hematite are all excellent choices. Hold the crystal in your hand while meditating or simply carry it with you throughout the day to promote balance and stability.

4. Essential Oils:

Essential oils like patchouli, cedarwood, and sandalwood can be incredibly helpful for balancing the Root Chakra. You can diffuse these oils in your home or mix a few drops with a carrier oil and apply them directly to the skin.

5. Nature walks:

Taking a walk in nature can also be incredibly grounding and beneficial for balancing the Root Chakra. Connect with the earth by taking off your shoes and walking barefoot in the grass. Pay attention to the sounds, smells, and sensations around you. Allow yourself to be present in the moment and feel your Root Chakra become more balanced and stable.

Incorporating these techniques into your daily routine can help you feel more grounded, stable, and secure. Practice with different strategies and find the best one for you. With a balanced Root Chakra, you'll feel more rooted and connected to the world around you.

Daily Practices for Strengthening the Root Chakra

Incorporating daily practices into your routine can help you strengthen and balance your Root Chakra, allowing you to feel more grounded and stable. Here are a few practices to try:

1. Practice Mindful Breathing: Deep breathing exercises can help you calm your mind and connect with your body. Start by taking deep, slow breaths, focusing on the sensation of the air moving in and out of your body. You can also try counting your breaths to help you stay focused.

2. Get Moving: Physical activity is a great way to release tension and boost your energy levels. Consider going for a walk or jog, doing some yoga, or trying low-impact exercises like swimming or cycling.

3. Connect with Nature: Spending time in nature can help you feel more grounded and connected. Take a walk in a park or nature reserve, go camping, or simply spend some time tending to plants in your garden.

4. Practice Gratitude: Gratitude can help you feel more positive and centered. Try keeping a gratitude journal, where you write down things you are grateful for each day. You can also take a few moments each day to reflect on the things in your life that bring you joy and contentment.

5. Eat Root Vegetables: Root vegetables like carrots, potatoes, and beets are said to be grounding and can help nourish your Root Chakra. Consider incorporating them into your meals as much as possible.

By incorporating these daily practices into your routine, you can strengthen and balance your Root Chakra, helping you feel more grounded and stable in your daily life. Remember that it's important to take care of yourself and prioritize your well-being.

Chapter 3: The Sacral Chakra: Creativity and Passion

Have you ever felt like your creativity was blocked or lacking? Struggling to come up with ideas or just feeling uninspired? In this chapter, we'll be exploring how to tap into and nurture your creativity through the power of the Sacral Chakra. The Sacral Chakra, located just below the navel, is associated with creativity, emotional intelligence, and passion. By understanding and aligning this energy center, you will be able to harness your creative potential and open yourself up to new and exciting possibilities. Keep reading to learn more about the Sacral Chakra and how to use it to access and enhance your creativity.

What is the Sacral Chakra?

Sacral chakras are associated with creativity, sexuality, and emotions and are located in the lower abdomen. It is believed to govern our sense of pleasure, joy, and passion in life, and is associated with the element of water.

The sacral chakra is responsible for our ability to be in touch with our own desires and to express ourselves creatively. It is also associated with our ability to connect with others in intimate and meaningful ways.

When the sacral chakra is balanced, we feel confident and able to express ourselves creatively without fear or self-doubt. We can experience pleasure and joy in our lives and can form deep, meaningful connections with others.

On the other hand, when the sacral chakra is imbalanced, we may struggle to express ourselves creatively or to feel pleasure in our lives. We may experience a sense of disconnection from our own emotions and desires or may struggle with issues related to intimacy and sexuality.

Balancing the sacral chakra can help us to tap into our creativity and passion in life and can help us to experience greater joy and fulfillment. By practicing techniques that support the sacral chakra, we can begin to unlock our full creative potential and live life more fully and authentically.

To open and balance the sacral chakra, it is important to become more aware of our emotions and cultivate a sense of self-love and self-acceptance. This can be achieved through a variety of practices, including meditation, yoga, and creative expression.

When we meditate on the sacral chakra, we focus on the area of the lower abdomen and visualize the chakra spinning and glowing with a bright, orange light. This helps to increase our awareness of our emotions and desires and to promote a sense of flow and ease in our lives.

Yoga poses such as the Pigeon pose and Cobra pose can also help to open and balance the sacral chakra. These poses help to increase blood flow to the area of the lower abdomen and can help to release any tension or blockages that may be preventing the flow of energy through the chakra.

Creative expression is also a powerful way to open and balance the sacral chakra. Engaging in activities such as painting, dancing, or writing can help to unleash our creativity and to connect us with our emotions and desires. By allowing ourselves to be vulnerable and to express ourselves authentically, we can begin to heal any wounds or blockages in the sacral chakra and to tap into our full creative potential.

By practicing techniques that support the sacral chakra, we can learn to harness our creativity and passion in life. By balancing this chakra, we can unlock our full potential and live life more fully and authentically.

The Importance of Creativity and Passion in Life

Creativity and passion are essential components of a happy and fulfilling life. Creativity is the expression of our innermost self, the manifestation of our unique ideas and talents. Passion is the fuel that drives us toward our goals, gives us purpose, and helps us find meaning in what we do.

Creativity is not limited to artistic endeavors alone, it is present in all aspects of our lives, from the way we decorate our homes to the way we solve problems at work. Being creative allows us to think outside the box, come up with innovative solutions, and explore new possibilities. It helps us develop a growth mindset, adapt to change, and overcome challenges.

Passion, on the other hand, is the spark that ignites our inner fire and motivates us to pursue our dreams. When we are passionate about something, we become more invested in it, put in extra effort, and are willing to take risks to achieve our goals. Passion also gives us a sense of purpose, direction, and fulfillment in life.

Without creativity and passion, life can become dull, monotonous, and unfulfilling. It is important to nurture these qualities within ourselves and cultivate them in our everyday lives. When we are creative and passionate, we are more engaged, energized, and optimistic about the future.

The Sacral Chakra is Linked to Sensuality and Sexuality

The sacral chakra is commonly known as the second chakra, and it's located in the lower abdomen. This chakra is associated with the element of water, and it's believed to be linked to our emotions, creativity, passion, sensuality, and sexuality.

Sensuality and sexuality are closely tied to the sacral chakra, as it's the center of our sexual and reproductive energy. This chakra is also linked to our ability to connect with others, to experience pleasure, and to embrace our own sexuality and sensuality.

When our sacral chakra is balanced, we're able to express ourselves creatively, we feel emotionally stable, and we're open to experiences of pleasure and joy. On the other hand, when our sacral chakra is blocked or imbalanced, we may struggle to connect with others, feel numb emotionally, or experience difficulties in our sex life.

Opening and balancing your sacral chakra can help you enhance your creativity and sensuality. Many practices can support the health of your sacral chakra, such as meditation, yoga, and working with crystals.

Incorporating daily rituals and practices that support your sacral chakra can help you connect more deeply with your sensuality and creativity, which can lead to greater satisfaction in your relationships, career, and overall well-being.

Signs of Imbalance in the Sacral Chakra

When your sacral chakra is out of balance, you may experience a range of physical, emotional, and mental symptoms that can disrupt your overall well-being. Here are some common signs of an imbalanced sacral chakra:

1. Lack of creativity: If you feel blocked creatively and struggle to come up with new ideas, it may indicate an imbalance in your sacral chakra. Your ability to express yourself creatively is closely linked to this energy center, and a blockage here can inhibit your imagination and make it difficult to tap into your innate creativity.

2. Emotional instability: The sacral chakra governs our emotions, and when it's out of balance, you may experience mood swings, anxiety, depression, or a lack of enthusiasm. You may feel disconnected from your emotions and struggle to express them effectively.

3. Reproductive and sexual issues: The sacral chakra is closely connected to our reproductive and sexual health. Imbalances in this energy center may manifest as fertility issues, menstrual problems, or low libido.

4. Addictive tendencies: An imbalanced sacral chakra can lead to addictive tendencies, as you may look for ways to numb or distract yourself from your emotional pain. You may turn to drugs, alcohol, or other substances to feel better, rather than addressing the underlying issues.

5. Poor relationships: As the sacral chakra governs our ability to connect with others on an emotional level, imbalances here can lead to difficulty in forming healthy relationships. You may struggle with intimacy or have trouble maintaining healthy boundaries.

If you're experiencing any of these symptoms, it's essential to focus on rebalancing your sacral chakra through various practices and techniques. In the next section, we'll discuss how you can open and balance this energy center to enhance your creativity and passion for life.

How to Open and Balance the Sacral Chakra for

Creative Expression

Now that we understand the importance of the Sacral Chakra for creative expression, let's explore ways to open and balance it.

1. Dance: Moving your body sensually and rhythmically is a great way to connect with the Sacral Chakra. Turn the music up and let yourself go freely, without judgment. This can help release any stuck energy and get your creative juices flowing.

2. Connect with Water: Water is associated with the Sacral Chakra. Take a bath or go for a swim, allowing the water to cleanse and purify your energy. This can also be a time for reflection and connecting with your emotions.

3. Practice Yoga: Certain yoga poses, such as hip openers and pelvic tilts, can stimulate the Sacral Chakra and increase creative energy. Some poses to try to include Goddess pose, Pigeon poses and the Cow face pose.

4. Create Art: Whether it's painting, drawing, writing, or another form of creative expression, allowing yourself to create without judgment can be incredibly healing for the Sacral Chakra. Set aside time each day to engage in your chosen form of art, even if it's just for a few minutes.

5. Embrace Your Sensuality: The Sacral Chakra is also linked to sensuality and sexuality. Taking the time to explore your body and connect with your senses can help open this energy center. This could include self-massage, wearing clothing that makes you feel good, among other ways.

By incorporating these practices into your daily routine, you can support your Sacral Chakra and enhance your creativity. Remember to listen to your body and honor your own unique process. With a balanced and open Sacral Chakra, you can tap into your full creative potential and live a more fulfilling life.

Practices to Support Your Sacral Chakra and Enhance Creativity

There are many practices you can incorporate into your daily routine to support your sacral chakra and enhance your creativity. Here are some ideas to get you started:

1. Journaling - Writing down your thoughts, feelings, and ideas can be a great way to tap into your creativity and release any pent-up emotions.

2. Dance - Sensually moving your body can help you connect with your sacral chakra and tap into your creativity. Try putting on some music and letting your body move freely.

3. Artistic expression - Whether it's painting, drawing, or crafting, allowing yourself to create without judgment can help you connect with your inner artist and express yourself more freely.

4. Sensual experiences - Engage your senses in pleasurable activities, such as taking a warm bath with essential oils or indulging in a delicious meal. These experiences can help you connect with your body and enhance your creativity.

5. Yoga - Certain yoga poses, such as pigeon pose or butterfly pose, can help open and balance your sacral chakra, while also promoting flexibility and relaxation.

6. Meditation - Take time to quiet your mind and focus on your breath, allowing yourself to become more present in the moment and connected with your creative energy.

Remember, there is no one "right" way to enhance your creativity or support your sacral chakra. The key is to listen to your body and find what works best for you. By taking the time to connect with your sacral chakra and explore your creativity, you may be surprised by the depth and richness that emerges in your life.

Chapter 4: A Guide to the Solar Plexus Chakra: Tapping into Your Inner Strength

Do you ever feel like you lack the confidence and inner strength to take on life's challenges? If so, you're not alone. Many of us struggle with a lack of personal power and feelings of insecurity. However, understanding and activating the Solar Plexus Chakra can help us to tap into our inner strength and foster greater self-confidence. In this chapter, we will explore the Solar Plexus Chakra and how it can be used to empower ourselves.

Understanding the Solar Plexus Chakra

This chakra governs personal power, self-confidence, and self-esteem and is located in the upper abdomen. It governs how we present ourselves to the world. It is the Solar Plexus Chakra that gives us a feeling of confidence and empowerment when it is balanced.

In addition to yellow's symbolism of warmth and optimism, the Solar Plexus Chakra is also associated with fire's symbolism of transformation and energy.

We feel empowered and self-sufficient when our Solar Plexus Chakra is open and balanced; we trust our instincts and feel in charge of our lives. A solar plexus chakra imbalance, however, can lead to feelings of insecurity, self-doubt, and low self-esteem.

We can use many healing and balancing techniques to align the Solar Plexus Chakra, such as meditation, yoga, and energy work, to cultivate self-worth and confidence. The Solar Plexus Chakra can also be empowered through affirmations and visualization techniques.

Your daily routine can help you tap into your inner strength and cultivate a sense of confidence and personal power by including practices that support your Solar Plexus Chakra.

The Solar Plexus Chakra is intimately connected to our digestive system and metabolism

A balanced Solar Plexus chakra aids in proper digestion, while an imbalance can cause digestive issues like bloating, constipation, or diarrhea. When the Solar Plexus Chakra is balanced, we feel energetic and full of vitality.

Signs of an imbalanced Solar Plexus Chakra include feelings of powerlessness, lack of motivation, self-doubt, anxiety, and depression. A balanced chakra promotes inner peace, confidence, and assertiveness.

To heal and balance the Solar Plexus Chakra, you can incorporate yoga poses like warrior and plank poses, as well as pranayama breathing techniques like kapalbhati and nadi shodhana. Meditation, visualization, and aromatherapy with essential oils like ginger, peppermint, and lemon can also aid in balancing the Solar Plexus Chakra.

Affirmations are another powerful way to empower the Solar Plexus Chakra. You can repeat affirmations like "I am confident and strong" or "I trust myself and my abilities" to help reinforce a positive self-image and self-worth.

Finally, incorporating Solar Plexus Chakra practices into your daily routine can help you tap into your inner strength and cultivate confidence and personal power. This can include practices like affirmations, meditation, yoga, or even just setting positive intentions for the day ahead. By regularly nurturing your Solar Plexus Chakra, you can cultivate a strong sense of self and move forward in life with confidence and purpose.

Characteristics of a Balanced Solar Plexus Chakra

When your Solar Plexus Chakra is balanced, you feel confident and empowered in yourself and your abilities. You trust your intuition and are able to make decisions with clarity and conviction. You feel a sense of inner strength and self-control, which helps you to manage your emotions and handle stressful situations with ease. People with balanced Solar Plexus Chakras have a strong sense of self and personal power, and they are able to achieve their goals and dreams with determination and focus.

Physically, a balanced Solar Plexus Chakra can manifest as good digestive health, healthy metabolism, and overall physical strength. Mentally, a balanced Solar Plexus Chakra can help you stay focused, motivated, and driven toward success in your personal and professional life. Emotionally, you are able to express yourself with confidence and assertiveness, without being aggressive or passive.

Overall, a balanced Solar Plexus Chakra allows you to tap into your inner strength and resilience, helping you to navigate through life's challenges with ease and grace.

If you want to cultivate a balanced Solar Plexus Chakra, it is important to practice self-care and self-love. Engage in activities that make you feel good about yourself and celebrate your achievements, big or small. When you take care of yourself, you create a strong foundation for your personal power and confidence to thrive.

Signs of an Imbalanced Solar Plexus Chakra

When your Solar Plexus Chakra is out of balance, it can manifest in a variety of ways. Some of the signs that you may have an imbalanced Solar Plexus Chakra include:

1. Lack of self-esteem: When your Solar Plexus Chakra is imbalanced, you may struggle with feeling confident and secure in yourself. This can lead to feelings of inadequacy and self-doubt.

2. Fear of rejection: If you find yourself constantly seeking approval from others, it could be a sign that your Solar Plexus Chakra is imbalanced. Risk-taking and pursuing your goals can be hindered by this fear of rejection.

3. Digestive issues: Digestion is closely linked to the Solar Plexus Chakra. Imbalances in this chakra can lead to digestive issues such as indigestion, bloating, and constipation.

4. Anger and frustration: An imbalanced Solar Plexus Chakra can also lead to feelings of anger and frustration. You may find yourself easily irritated or lashing out at others.

5. Lack of motivation: When your Solar Plexus Chakra is out of balance, you may struggle with motivation and finding the drive to pursue your goals and passions.

It's important to recognize these signs of an imbalanced Solar Plexus Chakra so that you can take steps to bring balance and healing to this area of your energy system.

Healing and Balancing Techniques for the Solar Plexus Chakra

When the Solar Plexus Chakra is imbalanced, you may experience feelings of powerlessness, lack of self-esteem, and low self-confidence. To restore balance and heal the Solar Plexus Chakra, there are several techniques you can practice:

Visualizations

A visualization is a powerful tool that can help you connect with the Solar Plexus Chakra and activate its energy. Sit comfortably in a quiet place, close your eyes, and imagine a bright yellow light emanating from your Solar Plexus. Picture the light growing brighter and more colorful as you breathe in. As you exhale, release any tension or negative energy from your body.

Yoga Poses

Certain yoga poses can help stimulate the Solar Plexus Chakra and release any blocked energy. These poses include the Warrior, Boat, and Cobra poses. Practicing these poses regularly can help restore balance to the Solar Plexus Chakra.

Crystal healing:

Several crystals can help balance and heal the Solar Plexus Chakra, including citrine, tiger's eye, and yellow topaz. Place the crystal on your Solar Plexus Chakra or wear it as a piece of jewelry to activate its healing properties.

Sound therapy:

Sound therapy involves using specific frequencies and vibrations to balance and restore energy flow. Listening to or chanting the mantra

"RAM" can help stimulate the Solar Plexus Chakra and activate its energy.

Essential Oils

Certain essential oils, such as lemon, grapefruit, and peppermint, can help stimulate the Solar Plexus Chakra and promote confidence and empowerment. Add a few drops of the essential oil to a diffuser or apply it topically to your Solar Plexus Chakra.

By practicing these techniques regularly, you can restore balance and harmony to your Solar Plexus Chakra and tap into your inner strength and personal power.

Affirmations to Empower the Solar Plexus Chakra

Affirmations are powerful tools to reprogram our subconscious mind and help us shift our mindset towards a more positive and empowered state.

Here are some affirmations that can help you activate and strengthen your Solar Plexus Chakra:

1. Success and abundance are worthy and deserving of me.

2. I trust my inner guidance and make decisions with confidence.

3. I am resilient and strong in the face of challenges.

4. I respect myself and others and set healthy boundaries.

5. I radiate positivity and confidence wherever I go.

6. I embrace change and take risks to achieve my goals.

7. I am grateful for all the opportunities and blessings in my life.

8. I release any fear, doubt or self-doubt that holds me back from my full potential.

9. It is possible for me to accomplish anything I set my mind to.10. I am powerful, creative and self-assured.

Repeat these affirmations to yourself daily, either in the morning or before going to bed. You can also write them down on a piece of paper and place it where you can see it often, such as your bathroom mirror or workspace. With time and consistency, these affirmations can help you boost your self-confidence, strengthen your willpower and achieve your goals with ease.

Incorporating Solar Plexus Chakra Practices into Your Daily Routine

Now that you have a deeper understanding of the solar plexus chakra, it's time to start incorporating some practices into your daily routine. Remember, a balanced solar plexus chakra can help you tap into your personal power and boost your confidence.

Here are some ways to do just that:

1. Practice mindful breathing: Set aside a few minutes each day to practice deep breathing. Simply breathe in deeply through your nose and breathe out through your mouth. Feel any tension or stress leaving your body as you exhale.

2. Move your body: Engage in physical activities that make you feel strong and powerful. This could be anything from yoga or Pilates to weightlifting or martial arts.

3. Express yourself: Take some time each day to express yourself creatively. Write in a journal, paint, or dance – whatever form of expression feels most authentic to you.

4. Set boundaries: Remember that saying "no" is a form of self-care. Be mindful of your energy levels and prioritize your own needs.

5. Practice positive self-talk: Acknowledge any self-deprecating statements or negative thoughts with positive affirmations to combat them. Repeat phrases like "I am capable," "I trust my instincts," and "I am confident" to yourself throughout the day.

Incorporating these practices into your daily routine can help you maintain a healthy and balanced solar plexus chakra. Remember, the more you prioritize your personal power and confidence, the more you'll be able to show up as your most authentic and empowered self in all areas of your life.

Chapter 5: The Heart Chakra: Love and Emotional Healing

The role of emotions in our lives is crucial. They shape our relationships, our attitudes, and our happiness. But how much do we really know about how our emotions work and the role that the heart chakra plays in our emotional well-being? In this chapter, we'll explore the heart chakra and how it impacts our emotional and spiritual health. We'll look at how to open and strengthen the heart chakra, how it relates to love, and what we can do to help ourselves heal emotionally. So get ready to open your heart and learn how to bring more love and emotional healing into your life.

Understanding the Heart Chakra

The heart chakra, also known as Anahata, is the fourth chakra in the body's chakra system. Green is the color associated with this chakra, located near the heart in the center of the chest. The heart chakra governs our ability to love and connect with ourselves, others, and the world around us.

The heart chakra is responsible for emotional balance and harmony. When our heart chakra is open and balanced, we are able to give and receive love freely, and we feel a deep sense of peace and contentment. This chakra is also responsible for our ability to feel empathy, compassion, and kindness towards others.

On the other hand, if our heart chakra is blocked or unbalanced, we may experience feelings of loneliness, sadness, and despair. We may find it difficult to trust others or struggle with developing healthy relationships. This can lead to a variety of physical, emotional, and psychological symptoms, including depression, anxiety, and physical pain.

Understanding the heart chakra is key to unlocking emotional healing and personal growth. By recognizing the importance of love and compassion, we can begin to connect with our heart chakra and cultivate a deeper sense of self-awareness and acceptance. This can help us overcome negative emotions and experiences, and foster positive, healthy relationships with ourselves and others.

The Connection Between the Heart Chakra and Emotional Healing

Our heart chakra is not only responsible for our physical heart, but it also plays a crucial role in our emotional well-being. This energy center is associated with the element of air and is located in the center of the chest, representing our capacity for love, compassion, and connection.

When our heart chakra is in balance, we feel a sense of inner peace and emotional stability. We are able to give and receive love freely and authentically, and we are more open to cultivating meaningful relationships with others. However, when our heart chakra is blocked or out of balance, it can manifest as emotional imbalances and cause feelings of sadness, anxiety, and loneliness.

The heart chakra is closely connected to our emotions, as it governs the energy flow between our physical and emotional bodies. By keeping our heart chakra balanced, we can enhance our ability to process and express our emotions effectively. When our heart chakra is balanced, we are more equipped to manage challenging situations with ease, respond to life's difficulties with resilience, and navigate relationships with greater understanding and compassion.

By nurturing our heart chakra, we are also able to cultivate greater empathy, compassion, and understanding towards others. When we are in tune with our own emotions and emotional needs, we become more aware and attentive to the emotional needs of others, enabling us to form more meaningful connections with those around us.

In summary, our heart chakra plays an integral role in our emotional well-being, and by keeping it in balance, we can enhance our capacity for love, connection, and compassion.

Signs of a Blocked Heart Chakra

A blocked heart chakra can manifest in various ways, impacting our emotional and physical well-being. Some common signs of a blocked heart chakra include:

1. Feeling disconnected from emotions: When the heart chakra is blocked, we may find it difficult to access and express our emotions. This can result in a sense of numbness or detachment from our feelings.

2. Lack of compassion and empathy: The heart chakra is associated with our ability to empathize and connect with others. If this chakra is blocked, we may struggle to feel compassion and empathy towards others, leading to feelings of isolation and loneliness.

3. Difficulty with self-love: The heart chakra is also linked to our relationship with ourselves. When this chakra is blocked, we may find it hard to practice self-love and care, leading to negative self-talk and feelings of unworthiness.

4. Holding grudges and resentment: A blocked heart chakra can lead to feelings of anger, bitterness, and resentment towards others. We may struggle to forgive and move on from past hurt, impacting our relationships and overall well-being.

5. Physical symptoms: The heart chakra is linked to the heart, lungs, and circulatory system. Physical symptoms of a blocked heart chakra can include chest pain, shortness of breath, and high blood pressure.

Recognizing these signs can be the first step towards opening and balancing the heart chakra and improving our emotional and physical health.

How to Open and Balance the Heart Chakra

If you're feeling stuck in negative emotions or struggling with relationships, it's possible that your Heart Chakra is blocked. But the good news is that with a few simple techniques, you can open and balance this chakra, which will improve your emotional well-being and overall happiness.

Here are some tips to get started:

1. Practice forgiveness: Holding grudges and resentments can weigh heavily on your heart. Practicing forgiveness towards yourself and others can help release these negative emotions and open your heart to love and compassion.

2. Practice heart-opening yoga poses: Yoga is an effective way to release tension and balance the energy in your chakras. Heart-opening poses like cobra, camel, and bridge pose are particularly helpful for the Heart Chakra.

3. Meditate on love and compassion: Take a few moments each day to meditate on the concepts of love and compassion. Visualize these emotions flowing in and out of your heart, filling you up with positive energy.

4. Use affirmations: Affirmations are a powerful tool for opening and balancing the Heart Chakra. Repeat positive statements like "I am worthy of love and belonging" or "I open myself to giving and receiving love" to help shift your mindset and energy.

5. Spend time in nature: Being in nature can help us connect with our heart and cultivate feelings of peace and joy. Take a walk in a park or sit by a body of water to soak up the healing energy of nature.

Remember, opening and balancing the Heart Chakra is an ongoing process. Incorporating these practices into your daily routine can help keep your heart open and flowing with positive energy. With time and practice, you can cultivate a deep sense of love and compassion for yourself and others.

Practicing Self-Love and Compassion

Self-love and compassion are integral parts of opening and balancing the heart chakra. This chakra is the center of love, connection, and compassion, not just for others but also for ourselves. When our heart chakra is blocked, we may feel unworthy of love and have low self-esteem. However, practicing self-love and compassion can help us heal and open up this vital chakra.

Here are some practices to cultivate self-love and compassion:

1. Mindfulness: Start by becoming more mindful of your thoughts and self-talk. Notice when negative self-talk arises and consciously choose to reframe it in a more positive light. Remind yourself of your worth and value, and treat yourself with the same kindness and compassion you would give to a dear friend.

2. Self-Care: Make self-care a priority in your life. Engage in activities that bring you joy and make you feel good, such as exercise, reading, taking a hot bath, or spending time in nature. By prioritizing your needs and well-being, you are showing yourself that you are deserving of love and care.

3. Gratitude: Focus on what you are grateful for in your life. Start a gratitude journal and write down at least three things each day that you are thankful for. By shifting your focus to the positive aspects of your life, you can cultivate a more positive mindset and increase your feelings of self-worth and love.

4. Forgiveness: Practice forgiveness towards yourself for any past mistakes or perceived shortcomings. Let go of any guilt or shame and choose to move forward with compassion and self-love. Remember, we are all human and imperfect, and it is through our mistakes that we learn and grow.

By practicing self-love and compassion, we can heal and balance our heart chakra and create a more fulfilling and loving relationship with ourselves. When we love ourselves, we are better equipped to love and connect with others, creating a positive ripple effect in our relationships and the world around us.

Cultivating Relationships with Others through the Heart Chakra

As the center of love and connection, the heart chakra plays a crucial role in our relationships with others. When the heart chakra is balanced and open, we are able to cultivate healthy, supportive relationships that enrich our lives and bring us joy. On the other hand, when the heart chakra is blocked or closed off, we may struggle to form close bonds with others, experience loneliness, and struggle with trust issues.

So how can we use the heart chakra to build stronger relationships with those around us? One of the first steps is to cultivate a sense of empathy and compassion toward others. When we open our hearts to those around us, we are better able to understand their perspectives and experiences. This can lead to deeper connections and a greater sense of understanding and trust between us.

Another key component of using the heart chakra to improve our relationships is to practice forgiveness. Holding onto grudges and resentments can weigh heavily on our hearts, causing us to close ourselves off from others. By practicing forgiveness and letting go of anger and hurt, we can create space for love and connection to thrive.

Finally, it's important to prioritize communication and honesty in our relationships. When we can speak openly and honestly with those around us, we are able to build trust and deepen our connections. By staying present and engaged in our relationships, we can use the power of the heart chakra to create meaningful and fulfilling connections with those around us.

Chapter 6: The Throat Chakra: Authentic Expression and Communication

Have you ever felt like you needed to express yourself but couldn't find the words? Or maybe you feel like you're stuck in a loop of negative self-talk that's holding you back from reaching your full potential. Understanding the power of authentic expression can help you unlock your true potential and live a more fulfilled life. In this chapter, we'll explore the importance of the throat chakra and how it relates to authentic expression and communication. We'll also learn how to open and balance the throat chakra for improved communication and connection.

What is the Throat Chakra?

The Throat Chakra, also known as Vishuddha, is located at the center of the throat and is associated with communication, self-expression, and creativity. This chakra is responsible for our ability to articulate our thoughts and feelings, as well as listen to others. It allows us to connect with others and express our authentic selves without fear or hesitation.

The Throat Chakra is also associated with our ability to connect with our inner truth and spiritual awareness. When this chakra is in balance, we feel confident and empowered in expressing our true selves and can communicate effectively and empathetically with others.

However, if this chakra is blocked or imbalanced, it can lead to physical and emotional symptoms. It is essential to keep this chakra in balance for overall physical, emotional, and spiritual well-being.

The Throat Chakra governs the thyroid gland, which regulates our metabolism and energy levels. When this chakra is blocked, it can manifest physically in issues such as sore throat, neck pain, dental problems, and thyroid imbalances. On an emotional level, an imbalanced Throat Chakra can lead to feelings of insecurity, fear of rejection, social anxiety, and difficulty expressing oneself authentically.

To balance and heal your Throat Chakra, there are various methods you can try. These include meditation, energy healing, yoga poses, and using affirmations specific to the chakra. Additionally, you can work on strengthening your communication skills, such as active listening and using "I" statements instead of accusatory language.

Some tools that can help you improve your communication skills include reading books on effective communication, attending workshops or therapy, and practicing with a trusted friend or partner. There are also many exercises you can do to strengthen your throat chakra and improve your communication abilities, such as chanting, singing, and writing in a journal.

Overall, understanding the Throat Chakra and its importance in authentic expression and communication can greatly benefit your overall well-being. By balancing and healing this chakra, you can improve your ability to communicate effectively and connect with others on a deeper level.

The importance of Authentic Expression

The throat chakra, or Vishuddha, is the center for communication, self-expression, and creativity. It is located in the throat and governs the mouth, tongue, and neck. The throat chakra helps us express ourselves honestly and clearly, and when it is balanced, we are able to communicate our needs, feelings, and thoughts effectively.

Authentic expression is crucial for our mental and emotional wellbeing, as it allows us to connect with others, build healthy relationships, and achieve our goals. However, many of us struggle with expressing ourselves authentically, often due to fear, anxiety, or past traumas.

When the throat chakra is blocked or imbalanced, it can manifest in physical symptoms such as a sore throat, thyroid problems, and difficulty swallowing or speaking. Emotionally, an imbalanced throat chakra can lead to difficulty expressing oneself, a fear of public speaking, and a lack of confidence.

Learning how to balance and heal your throat chakra can help you connect with your authentic voice and improve your communication skills. Some practices that can help include meditation, breathwork, yoga, and journaling. These practices can help you connect with your inner self, release pent-up emotions, and gain a deeper understanding of your communication patterns.

In addition to these practices, there are also tools you can use to strengthen your communication skills, such as active listening, clear communication, and assertiveness. These tools can help you communicate effectively and avoid misunderstandings or conflicts in your relationships.

One helpful practice for improving communication skills is to practice empathy and active listening. When we actively listen to someone, we are fully present and focused on what they are saying, without interrupting or judging. This can help us understand their perspective and communicate more effectively.

Another practice is to use "I" statements, which can help us communicate our needs and feelings without blaming or attacking others. For example, instead of saying "You always make me feel like I'm not important," you could say "I feel ignored when you don't listen to me."

By understanding the importance of authentic expression and developing our communication skills, we can connect more deeply with ourselves and others and live more fulfilling lives.

Physical symptoms of a blocked throat chakra

When the throat chakra is blocked, it can manifest as physical symptoms in the neck, throat, and other parts of the body. Here are some common signs that your throat chakra may be blocked:

1. Sore throat: A persistent sore throat that does not respond to medication or other treatments can be a sign of an imbalanced throat chakra.

2. Neck pain: If you are experiencing pain or stiffness in your neck, it may be related to a blockage in your throat chakra.

3. Hoarseness or loss of voice: When your throat chakra is blocked, it can affect your ability to speak clearly, causing hoarseness or a loss of voice.

4. Thyroid problems: The thyroid gland, which is located in the neck, is closely connected to the throat chakra. A blockage in the throat chakra can affect the functioning of the thyroid gland, leading to a range of thyroid problems.

5. Headaches: Blockages in the throat chakra can cause tension headaches that often radiate from the neck to the back of the head.

6. Jaw pain: If you experience pain or stiffness in your jaw, it may be related to a blockage in your throat chakra.

If you are experiencing any of these physical symptoms, it is important to consult with a healthcare professional to rule out any underlying medical conditions. At the same time, you can also work on balancing and healing your throat chakra through a variety of techniques, such as meditation, sound healing, and energy healing. By releasing any blockages in your throat chakra, you can restore your ability to communicate clearly and express yourself authentically.

Emotional signs of an imbalanced throat chakra

In addition to physical symptoms, an imbalanced throat chakra can manifest in a variety of emotional ways. These signs may include difficulty speaking up for oneself, feeling misunderstood, fear of rejection or criticism, and lack of confidence in one's communication skills.

When our throat chakra is not functioning optimally, we may struggle to express ourselves clearly, leading to feelings of frustration or dissatisfaction in our relationships and interactions with others. On the other hand, an overactive throat chakra may result in excessive talking or interrupting others, dominating conversations and failing to listen effectively

.

It's important to note that these emotional symptoms may also be related to other chakras, and it's essential to take a holistic approach to healing and balancing all of our energy centers. However, focusing on the throat chakra can be especially helpful for improving communication and strengthening relationships with those around us.

By addressing these emotional imbalances, we can work towards creating more harmonious interactions with others, expressing our true selves, and feeling more confident in our ability to communicate effectively. In the next section, we will explore ways to balance and heal our throat chakra.

How to balance and heal your throat chakra

If you feel like your throat chakra is blocked or imbalanced, don't worry, there are ways to heal and balance it. Here are some methods you can try:

1. Chanting or singing: The sound vibrations created by chanting or singing can help to clear blockages in your throat chakra and balance it. You can try chanting mantras such as "OM" or singing along to your favorite songs.

2. Essential oils: Essential oils like lavender, peppermint, and chamomile have calming and soothing effects that can help to open and balance your throat chakra. You can diffuse them in your room or add a few drops to your bathwater.

3. Mindful breathing: Focusing on your breath can help to release any tension in your throat and balance your chakra. Take a few deep breaths and visualize the air moving freely through your throat.

4. Yoga: Certain yoga poses, such as the shoulder stand and fish pose, can help to stimulate and balance your throat chakra. Find a yoga class or practice at home using a yoga app.

5. Blue foods: Eating blue foods, such as blueberries and blackberries, can help to stimulate and balance your throat chakra. They also contain antioxidants that are beneficial for overall health.

By incorporating these practices into your daily routine, you can work towards healing and balancing your throat chakra and improve your ability to communicate effectively. Remember that it's important to listen to your body and seek professional help if you experience any persistent physical or emotional symptoms.

Tools for strengthening your communication

skills

In addition to balancing and healing your throat chakra, there are several tools and techniques you can use to strengthen your communication skills. These tools can help you express yourself more authentically, listen more effectively, and connect with others on a deeper level.

1. Active Listening: One of the most powerful communication tools is active listening. This involves giving your full attention to the person speaking, asking clarifying questions, and reflecting back on what you hear to ensure that you understand. Active listening helps to create a safe and supportive space for communication.

2. Mindful Communication: Mindful communication is the practice of speaking and listening with intention, presence, and awareness. This involves being mindful of your own thoughts and emotions, as well as those of the person you are communicating with. Misunderstandings, conflicts, and miscommunications can be reduced through mindful communication.

3. Nonviolent Communication: Marshall Rosenberg developed nonviolent communication as a method of communication. It involves expressing yourself with honesty and empathy and listening with compassion and understanding. Nonviolent communication helps to promote mutual understanding and respect and can help to resolve conflicts and build stronger relationships.

4. Assertiveness Training: Assertiveness training can help you to communicate your needs and boundaries clearly and confidently. This involves learning how to say "no" when necessary, how to express your opinions and feelings, and how to make requests respectfully and effectively.

5. Public Speaking: For developing communication skills, public speaking is an invaluable resource. It involves speaking in front of an audience and conveying a message with clarity and confidence. Public speaking can help you to overcome fears and insecurities around communication and can help you to develop more effective speaking skills.

By using these tools and techniques, you can strengthen your communication skills and become a more confident and effective communicator. Remember that communication is a skill that can be developed and improved with practice, so don't be afraid to try new things and step out of your comfort zone.

Practice exercises to improve your ability to communicate effectively.

Just like any other skill, effective communication takes practice. Here are a few exercises you can try to improve your ability to express yourself authentically and communicate effectively:

1. Journaling: Writing down your thoughts and feelings in a journal can help you become more comfortable with expressing yourself honestly. It can also give you clarity and insight into your own communication patterns.

2. Mirror work: Stand in front of a mirror and practice speaking out loud. Focus on maintaining eye contact with yourself and speak slowly and clearly. This exercise can help build confidence in your ability to express yourself and also help with public speaking.

3. Active listening: Practice really listening to others when they speak. This means being fully present, giving your full attention and not interrupting. This not only helps you become a better listener but also helps to build stronger relationships.

4. Mindfulness meditation: Mindfulness practices such as meditation can help you become more aware of your thoughts and emotions, which can help you communicate more clearly and effectively. You can start by spending just a few minutes a day and gradually increase your time.

5. Conflict resolution exercises: Conflict is a natural part of any relationship. Learning how to navigate it healthily is important for effective communication. Practice exercises like "I" statements and active listening to help resolve conflicts and communicate effectively.

By practicing these exercises regularly, you can strengthen your throat chakra and improve your communication skills, leading to more authentic relationships and better outcomes in your personal and professional life.

Chapter 7: The Third Eye Chakra: Intuition and Inner Wisdom

Do you ever feel like you have a sixth sense for knowing when something is off, or that you can "sense" things that others may not be aware of? If so, then you are likely already tapping into your Third Eye Chakra, the energetic center of intuition and inner wisdom. In this blog post, we'll explore the Third Eye Chakra and discuss how you can develop and expand your connection to your intuitive and higher self.

What is the Third Eye Chakra?

In Sanskrit, the third eye chakra is called the Ajna chakra and is situated between the eyebrows in the forehead. It is associated with spirituality, insight, and intuition.

A lotus flower with two petals represents the dualistic nature of the mind, while a light-blue triangle represents the inner guidance and wisdom found within.

A balanced third eye chakra allows us to trust our intuition, perceive the truth beyond what our senses tell us, and understand ourselves and the world more deeply. It is possible, however, to experience confusion, anxiety, and difficulty making decisions if your third eye chakra is blocked or overactive.

We will explore the characteristics of an open third eye chakra, signs of an imbalanced third eye chakra, and practices to balance and activate this important energy center in the following sections.

Characteristics of an Open Third Eye Chakra

When your Third Eye Chakra is open and balanced, you will experience several characteristics that are related to your intuition and inner wisdom.

Here are some of the signs of an open Third Eye Chakra:

1. Intuition: You trust your inner guidance and have a strong sense of intuition. You may experience a gut feeling or a sudden insight that helps you make decisions.

2. Clarity: You have a clear and focused mind that is not easily distracted. You can see through illusions and perceive the truth behind things.

3. Vision: You have a strong visualization ability and can visualize your goals and dreams. Additionally, one can visualize concepts or abstractions not present in physical space.

4. Imagination: You have a vivid imagination and can come up with creative solutions to problems.

5. Wisdom: You have access to your inner wisdom and can make wise decisions. You are also open to learning and growing.

6. Connection: You feel a strong connection to your higher self and the universe. You may experience synchronicities or a sense of being guided.

7. Spiritual Awareness: You have a heightened sense of spiritual awareness and can see beyond the physical world. You may experience spiritual visions or have psychic abilities.

If you experience any of these characteristics, it is a sign that your Third Eye Chakra is open and functioning well. However, if you struggle with any of these areas, your Third Eye Chakra may be blocked or overactive. In the next section, we will discuss the signs of a blocked or overactive Third Eye Chakra.

Signs of a Blocked or Overactive Third Eye Chakra

An imbalanced Third Eye Chakra can affect your physical, mental, and emotional well-being.

Here are some signs that your Third Eye Chakra may be blocked or overactive:

Blocked Third Eye Chakra:

- Feeling disconnected from your intuition and inner wisdom

making decisions or trusting your instincts is difficult- Lack of imagination and creativity

- Poor memory and inability to concentrate

- Feeling disoriented or confused

- Headaches or migraines

- Sinus or eye problems

Overactive Third Eye Chakra:

- Overly relying on intuition and neglecting practical considerations

- Constantly living in a dream world and ignoring reality

- Being too critical or judgmental of yourself and others

- Experiencing hallucinations or delusions

- Feeling overwhelmed or anxious

- Insomnia or other sleep disorders

- Headaches or migraines

If you notice any of these symptoms, it's a sign that your Third Eye Chakra needs balancing and activation. Fortunately, there are various practices and techniques you can use to open up and stimulate this chakra.

In the next section, we will discuss some practices to balance and activate the Third Eye Chakra.

Practices to Balance and Activate the Third Eye Chakra

The third eye chakra is connected with intuition, personal insight, and intuitive wisdom. Balancing and activating this chakra can help us tap into our intuition, access our inner guidance, and enhance our spiritual experiences.

Here are some practices that can help balance and activate the Third Eye Chakra:

1. Meditation: Meditation is an effective way to activate the Third Eye Chakra. Sit in a quiet and peaceful place and focus your attention on the space between your eyebrows. Visualize a purple light in this area, and imagine it expanding and filling your entire body with its healing energy.

2. Yoga: Certain yoga postures can also help activate the Third Eye Chakra. Practice postures such as Downward-Facing Dog, Child's Pose, and Eagle Pose to stimulate the Third Eye Chakra.

3. Affirmations: Affirmations are positive statements that can help shift our thoughts and beliefs. Repeat affirmations such as "I trust my intuition," "I am connected to my inner wisdom," or "I have access to spiritual insight" to activate and balance your Third Eye Chakra.

4. Essential Oils: Essential oils such as frankincense, sandalwood, and lavender can help stimulate and balance the Third Eye Chakra. Diffuse these oils or apply them to the Third Eye Chakra area during meditation or throughout the day.

5. Journaling: Writing down your thoughts and feelings can help you connect with your inner wisdom and intuition. Set aside time to journal daily and reflect on any intuitive insights you may receive.

By practicing these techniques, you can balance and activate your Third Eye Chakra, connect with your inner wisdom, and enhance your spiritual experiences.

Meditation for Third Eye Chakra Activation

Meditation is a powerful tool to activate and balance the Third Eye Chakra. This is how you do a Third Eye Chakra meditation:

1. Find a quiet and peaceful place where you can sit comfortably with your spine straight.

2. Take a few deep breaths to relax your body and clear your mind.

3. Close your eyes and focus your attention to the area between your eyebrows.

4. Imagine a beautiful indigo light glowing and expanding from your Third Eye Chakra.

5. Visualize this light becoming brighter and brighter, filling your whole body with its powerful energy.

6. Take a few deep breaths, inhaling this light and exhaling any negative energy or thoughts.

7. Repeat the affirmation: "I trust my inner wisdom and intuition. I am open to receiving divine guidance and insights."

8. Stay in this meditation for as long as you like, allowing yourself to connect with your inner wisdom and intuition.

9. When you're ready, gently open your eyes and take a few moments to ground yourself before returning to your daily activities.

Remember, regular meditation practice can help you strengthen your Third Eye Chakra and develop a deeper connection with your inner wisdom and intuition.

Connecting with Your Inner Wisdom

Our inner wisdom is a powerful tool that allows us to make the best decisions in our lives. It helps us understand our true purpose, motivates us to take action, and guides us towards our dreams and aspirations. However, to connect with our inner wisdom, we need to first activate and balance our Third Eye Chakra.

Here are some practices that can help you connect with your inner wisdom:

1. Practice mindfulness: Mindfulness helps you tune in to your body, thoughts, and emotions. It helps you be aware of your surroundings, and make informed decisions. Regular practice of mindfulness can help you connect with your inner wisdom.

2. Listen to your body: Your body has an innate wisdom that is connected to your intuition. Listen to the subtle signals that your body sends you, such as stomach aches, headaches, or even tingling sensations in certain parts of your body. These signals can provide important information about what you need to do or not do.

3. Journaling: Writing down your thoughts and feelings can help you connect with your inner wisdom. It can help you identify patterns in your life, understand your thoughts and emotions, and reflect on your actions.

4. Connect with nature: Spending time in nature can help you connect with your inner wisdom. Nature has a way of slowing down our minds, helping us focus on the present moment, and connecting us to something greater than ourselves.

5. Ask for guidance: Lastly, don't be afraid to ask for guidance from your inner wisdom, the universe, or a higher power. When you ask for guidance, you open yourself up to receive messages that can help you make the best decisions in your life.

Connecting with your inner wisdom is an ongoing practice, but with regular dedication and effort, it can help you lead a more fulfilling and purposeful life. Trust in yourself, and let your inner wisdom guide you towards the path of your dreams.

Using Your Intuition in Daily Life

Your intuition is your inner voice, guiding you towards what is right and true. It's your sixth sense, helping you make decisions and navigate through life's challenges. The Third Eye Chakra is the gateway to your intuition and inner wisdom, and it's important to develop this chakra to strengthen your intuition.

Here are some ways you can use your intuition in daily life:

1. Listen to Your Gut Feeling: When faced with a decision, listen to your gut feeling. Often, your intuition will guide you toward the best path to take.

2. Pay Attention to Signs and Synchronicities: Signs and synchronicities are messages from the universe, and they often come to us when we're in tune with our intuition. Keep an open mind and pay attention to the signs around you.

3. Trust Your Inner Voice: Your intuition speaks to you through your inner voice. Trust this voice, even if it goes against logic or reason.

4. Use Your Intuition in Relationships: Your intuition can help you navigate relationships, whether it's romantic or professional. Pay attention to how you feel around others and trust your instincts.

5. Use Your Intuition for Self-Reflection: Your intuition can guide you towards greater self-awareness and self-discovery. Use it to reflect on your thoughts, feelings, and behaviors.

Remember, developing your intuition is a process, and it takes time and practice. Use these tips to strengthen your intuition and connect with your inner wisdom. When you trust your intuition, you'll find that you're able to make decisions with greater clarity and confidence.

Chapter 8: The Crown Chakra: Divine Connection and Spiritual Awakening

Have you ever felt an inexplicable connection with the divine? If so, the answer may lie in your Crown Chakra. The Crown Chakra is the seventh of the major energy centers in the human body and is associated with spiritual enlightenment and connection with the divine. In this chapter, we'll discuss what the Crown Chakra is, how it functions, and how to open and balance it to bring you closer to the divine.

What is the Crown Chakra?

Crown Chakra, or Sahasrara, is the top chakra in the human body's energetic system. It is located at the top of the head, and its color is violet or white. The Crown Chakra is associated with spiritual enlightenment, divine connection, and self-realization. When this chakra is open and balanced, we feel a deep sense of spiritual connection and inner peace.

The Crown Chakra is said to be the seat of the soul, connecting us to the universal consciousness and the divine. It is the center of our intuition and wisdom, enabling us to understand the interconnectedness of all things. The Crown Chakra governs our higher mental functions, such as self-awareness, creativity, and insight.

In essence, the Crown Chakra is the gateway to the divine. It is through this chakra that we connect to our higher selves and the universe beyond. Opening and balancing this chakra is essential for spiritual growth and enlightenment.

Understanding the Crown Chakra's Role in

Spiritual Awakening

Crown chakras, also called Sahasrara chakras, are the seventh and highest chakras in the human energy system. It is located at the top of the head and is associated with the color violet or white. The Crown Chakra governs our connection with the divine and spiritual awakening.

When the Crown Chakra is balanced, it allows us to tap into our higher consciousness and connect with the divine. This connection helps us to understand the universe and our place in it, and it gives us a sense of purpose and meaning in life.

On the other hand, when the Crown Chakra is blocked, we may feel disconnected from the divine, ourselves, and the world around us. This disconnection can lead to feelings of isolation, depression, and confusion.

To open and balance the Crown Chakra, it is important to engage in practices that connect us with our higher selves and the divine. Some effective techniques include meditation, yoga, prayer, and visualization. These practices can help us to clear our minds and allow for a deeper connection with our inner selves and the universe.

Spiritual awakening occurs when we become aware of our true selves and our connection to the universe. It is a process of letting go of the ego and embracing a deeper, more meaningful existence. The Crown Chakra is the gateway to spiritual awakening, and balancing and opening it can help us to connect with the divine and experience spiritual growth.

Signs of a Blocked Crown Chakra

When your Crown Chakra is blocked or unbalanced, you may experience several physical, emotional, and spiritual symptoms. Here are some of the signs that indicate a blocked Crown Chakra:

1. Lack of Spiritual Connection: When a Crown Chakra is blocked, one of the primary symptoms may be a sense of being disconnected from your spiritual side. You may feel lost or disconnected from your inner self, as well as the Divine or Universe.

2. Difficulty Concentrating: A blocked Crown Chakra may also lead to difficulty concentrating, focusing, and understanding complex ideas.

3. Mental Confusion: You may experience confusion and indecisiveness about what you want in life, your purpose, or your place in the world.

4. Feeling Disconnected: A blocked Crown Chakra can leave you feeling isolated, aloof, or disconnected from the people around you.

5. Lack of Creativity: Your Crown Chakra also plays a crucial role in stimulating your creativity, imagination, and inspiration. A blocked Crown Chakra can hinder your creative energy, leading to a lack of inspiration and artistic abilities.

6. Headaches and Migraines: Another physical symptom of a blocked Crown Chakra is recurrent headaches or migraines, particularly around the top of your head.

7. Insomnia and Sleeping Issues: The Crown Chakra's imbalance can affect your sleep patterns, leading to insomnia or interrupted sleep.

If you notice these symptoms in yourself, it's essential to address your Crown Chakra's imbalances and seek methods to rebalance it.

Techniques for Balancing and Healing the Crown Chakra

When the Crown Chakra is blocked or out of balance, it can lead to feelings of disconnectedness, a lack of purpose, and a lack of spiritual growth. Here are some techniques you can use to balance and heal the Crown Chakra:

1. Meditation: Meditation is one of the most effective ways to balance and heal the Crown Chakra. Focus on the Crown Chakra during meditation and visualize it as a glowing violet or white light. This will help to open the chakra and connect you to the divine.

2. Yoga: Certain yoga postures, such as headstands and shoulder stands, can stimulate the Crown Chakra. Focus on your breath during these poses and visualize the flow of energy moving through your body and up to the Crown Chakra.

3. Sound Healing: The Crown Chakra resonates with the sound of "Om". Chanting or listening to this sound can help to balance and heal the chakra.

4. Crystals: Crystals such as amethyst, clear quartz, and selenite are all great for balancing and healing the Crown Chakra. When you meditate or carry them throughout the day, place them on your Crown Chakra.5. Aromatherapy: Essential oils such as lavender, frankincense, and sandalwood can help to balance and heal the Crown Chakra. Diffuse these oils during meditation or wear them as a perfume.

Remember, a balanced and healed Crown Chakra is crucial for connecting with the divine and experiencing spiritual growth. Incorporate these techniques into your daily routine and you will start to notice a difference in how you feel.

The Importance of Connecting with the Divine through the Crown Chakra

The Crown Chakra is the gateway to the divine, connecting us to a higher consciousness and spiritual realm. This energy center is responsible for our connection to a higher power and serves as a portal to higher knowledge and understanding.

When the Crown Chakra is balanced and open, we experience a sense of enlightenment and spiritual fulfillment. We can tap into our inner wisdom, intuition, and higher consciousness, leading us toward a path of growth and self-awareness.

Connecting with the divine through the Crown Chakra allows us to let go of limiting beliefs and patterns that hold us back from achieving our full potential. By surrendering to a higher power and embracing the unknown, we open ourselves up to endless possibilities and experiences.

Moreover, the Crown Chakra allows us to connect with a deeper sense of purpose and meaning in our lives. We become more aware of our place in the world and how we can contribute to something greater than ourselves.

Incorporating practices such as meditation, prayer, and gratitude into our daily routine can help us open and balance the Crown Chakra, leading to a more profound connection with the divine.

Incorporating Crown Chakra Practices into Your Daily Routine

If you're looking to connect more deeply with the divine and experience spiritual awakening, incorporating Crown Chakra practices into your daily routine can be a powerful tool. Here are some techniques to get you started:

1. Meditation: Sit in a quiet space and focus on the top of your head, where the Crown Chakra is located. Imagine a bright, white light pouring into your crown, filling your body with positive energy and connecting you to the divine.

2. Yoga: Practicing yoga postures that open up the top of the head, like the Headstand or Tree Pose, can stimulate the Crown Chakra.

3. Mantra Chanting: Chanting mantras like "Om" or "Aum" can help activate the Crown Chakra and promote spiritual connection.

4. Gratitude: Expressing gratitude for the blessings in your life can help open up the Crown Chakra and create a positive mindset.

5. Spend Time in Nature: Being in nature can help calm the mind, clear negative energy, and connect you with the divine.

Incorporating these practices into your daily routine can help you maintain balance in the Crown Chakra and stay connected to the divine. By doing so, you'll experience a sense of spiritual awakening and a deeper connection to your purpose and meaning in life.

The Crown Chakra is closely tied to higher states of consciousness and mystical experiences

As the highest chakra in the body, the Crown Chakra is associated with spiritual transcendence and the attainment of higher states of consciousness. When this chakra is open and balanced, it allows us to tap into our deepest spiritual truths, connect with the divine, and experience mystical states of awareness.

Through the Crown Chakra, we can experience a profound sense of unity with all things and a heightened sense of spiritual awareness.

This can lead to transformative experiences that open up new vistas of understanding and awareness.

However, when the Crown Chakra is blocked or imbalanced, it can result in a sense of disconnection from our spirituality and a lack of access to higher states of consciousness. Symptoms of an imbalanced Crown Chakra may include feelings of depression, anxiety, and disconnection from one's sense of purpose and spirituality.

To unlock the full potential of the Crown Chakra and experience the profound benefits it has to offer, it is essential to engage in practices that balance and heal this vital energy center. Techniques such as meditation, mindfulness, and breathwork can all be highly effective in this regard.

By making a concerted effort to engage with the Crown Chakra and integrate it into our daily lives, we can experience the profound sense of spiritual connectedness and inner peace that comes with a healthy and balanced Crown Chakra. Whether through yoga, meditation, prayer, or other practices, the journey of spiritual awakening begins with connecting with this vital energy center and exploring its full potential.

Chapter 9: Integration and Wholeness: Balancing the Chakra System

Are you feeling out of balance? Do you feel like your energy system is off-kilter? Rebalancing your chakras can help bring harmony and integration to your energy system. In this chapter, we'll discuss how the chakra system works and explore various techniques for rebalancing the chakras. With some focused attention and the right tools, you can achieve a sense of harmony and wholeness within yourself.

Understanding the Chakra System

The chakra system is a complex energy network within the body that has been recognized and studied for thousands of years in various cultures. It consists of seven main chakras located along the spine from the base to the crown of the head, each corresponding to specific physical, emotional, and spiritual aspects of our being.

The chakras are like spinning wheels of energy, and they need to be in balance and aligned for us to feel healthy, centered, and connected to our inner selves. When our chakras are out of balance or blocked, we can experience a range of physical and emotional symptoms, from digestive issues to anxiety, from lack of creativity to a feeling of disconnectedness.

In order to achieve balance and harmony within our chakra system, it's important to understand what each chakra represents and how it affects us. By learning to identify imbalances and practicing specific techniques to rebalance them, we can improve our overall well-being and sense of wholeness.

The seven chakras are as follows:

1. Root Chakra - represents our foundation, sense of security, and survival instincts

2. Sacral Chakra - represents our creativity, sexuality, and emotional balance

3. Solar Plexus Chakra - represents our personal power, self-confidence, and self-worth

4. Heart Chakra - represents our ability to love and connect with others, as well as ourselves

5. Throat Chakra - represents our communication and self-expression

6. Third Eye Chakra - represents our intuition and perception of the world

7. Crown Chakra - represents our connection to the divine and spiritual consciousness

By understanding these different aspects, we can begin to pinpoint which chakras may need extra attention and care. In the following sections, we will discuss some common signs of imbalanced chakras and specific techniques for rebalancing each chakra. Remember that these techniques can be combined and customized based on your own needs and preferences. The most important thing is to approach the practice with an open mind and heart, and to trust your intuition in finding what works best for you.

Signs of Imbalanced Chakras

The chakra system plays a significant role in our physical, emotional, and spiritual well-being. When our chakras are imbalanced or blocked, it can cause a variety of physical and emotional issues. Here are some common signs of imbalanced chakras to look out for:

1. Root Chakra: Feeling disconnected from your body, lacking a sense of safety and security, feeling anxious or fearful.

2. Sacral Chakra: Feeling emotionally numb, lacking creativity, struggling with addiction or unhealthy behaviors, and having low libido.

3. Solar Plexus Chakra: Struggling with low self-esteem, feeling powerless or insecure, lacking direction in life, struggling with digestive issues.

4. Heart Chakra: Struggling to form meaningful connections with others, feeling emotionally closed off, lacking empathy and compassion.

5. Throat Chakra: Struggling to express yourself, feeling anxious about public speaking, struggling to listen to others or communicate effectively.

6. Third Eye Chakra: Struggling to trust your intuition, feeling disconnected from your inner wisdom, lacking clarity or vision for your life.

7. Crown Chakra: Feeling disconnected from a higher power or source of spiritual guidance, struggling to find purpose, or meaning in life, lacking spiritual awareness.

If you notice any of these signs in your life, it may be time to take a closer look at your chakra system and work to rebalance any areas that are out of alignment. By doing so, you can improve your overall sense of well-being and find greater harmony in your energy system.

Fortunately, there are many techniques that can help you rebalance your chakras and restore harmony to your energy system. By using a combination of meditation, yoga, breathwork, visualization, and other practices, you can help unblock any stuck energy and bring your chakras back into balance. In the next sections, we will explore specific techniques for each of the seven chakras, starting with the root chakra. It's important to note that everyone's journey with chakra healing will be unique, and it's important to listen to your body and do what feels right for you. With consistent practice and patience, you can find greater balance and wholeness in your chakra system, leading to improved physical, emotional, and spiritual well-being.

Root Chakra Balancing Techniques

The Root Chakra, also known as the Muladhara Chakra, is located at the base of the spine and is responsible for grounding us to the earth. When this chakra is imbalanced, we may feel anxious, fearful, or disconnected from our bodies.

To balance the Root Chakra, there are several techniques that you can try:

1. Practice Grounding Exercises - One of the best ways to balance your Root Chakra is to practice grounding exercises. These may include walking barefoot in nature, gardening, or sitting on the earth with your legs crossed.

2. Incorporate Root Chakra Stones - Stones like red jasper, hematite, and garnet can help to balance your Root Chakra. Simply place these stones on your Root Chakra while you meditate or carry them with you throughout the day.

3. Try Yoga Poses - Yoga poses like the Warrior Pose, Mountain Pose, and Child's Pose can help to ground you and balance your Root Chakra.

4. Focus on Your Breath - Deep breathing exercises can also help to balance your Root Chakra. Try taking deep inhales and exhales, focusing on the sensation of your breath entering and leaving your body.

5. Use Affirmations - Affirmations can help to reprogram your mind and balance your Root Chakra. Try repeating affirmations like "I am safe", "I am grounded", and "I trust the universe" to help balance your energy system.

By incorporating these techniques into your daily routine, you can help to balance your Root Chakra and feel more grounded and connected to the earth. Remember to listen to your body and do what feels best for you. With patience and practice, you can find harmony in your energy system and experience greater balance and well-being in your life.

Sacral Chakra Balancing Techniques

The sacral chakra is the center of creativity, pleasure, and sexuality. When imbalanced, it can cause issues with intimacy, creativity, and emotional regulation. Luckily, there are many techniques you can use to balance your sacral chakra and bring harmony back to your energy system.

One simple way to balance your sacral chakra is to engage in activities that bring you joy and pleasure. This could be anything from dancing to listening to music to cooking a delicious meal. Whatever it is, make sure it's something that truly makes you happy and allows you to tap into your creativity.

Another technique is to practice pelvic exercises such as kegels. These exercises help to strengthen the muscles of the pelvic floor, which can improve sexual function and overall vitality in the sacral chakra.

Incorporating the color orange into your environment and wardrobe can also be helpful in balancing the sacral chakra. Orange is the color associated with this chakra and can help to stimulate its energy.

You may also want to consider working with healing crystals such as carnelian or orange calcite, which are said to help balance and energize the sacral chakra.

Finally, practicing mindfulness and meditation can help to balance all your chakras, including the sacral. Simply sitting quietly and focusing on your breath while visualizing the sacral chakra can help to bring it back into balance.

By incorporating these sacral chakra balancing techniques into your daily routine, you can help to bring harmony back to your energy system and enhance your creativity, pleasure, and overall well-being.

Solar Plexus Chakra Balancing Techniques

The solar plexus chakra is the center of personal power, willpower, and self-esteem. When this chakra is balanced, we feel confident, assertive, and able to take control of our lives. However, an imbalance in this chakra can lead to feelings of insecurity, self-doubt, and lack of confidence.

Here are some techniques to balance your solar plexus chakra:

Mindful Breathing:

Sit comfortably and take deep, slow breaths. Visualize golden light filling your solar plexus, as you inhale and exhale. This helps to activate and balance the chakra.

Physical Activities

Engage in physical activities such as running, swimming, or practicing yoga to stimulate the solar plexus chakra. These activities increase blood flow, which can help release any blockages.

Positive Affirmations

Recite positive affirmations such as "I am confident" or "I trust myself" to strengthen your self-esteem. Repeat them several times to internalize the message and shift any negative thought patterns.

Yellow Foods:

The solar plexus chakra is a source of warmth and emits the color yellow. Eating yellow fruits and vegetables such as bananas, lemons, and corn can help balance this chakra.

Sit in a quiet space, close your eyes, and focus on your solar plexus. Visualize a bright yellow ball of light in this area. Allow the light to expand and radiate throughout your body, energizing and balancing the chakra.

By practicing these techniques, you can balance your solar plexus chakra and feel more confident and in control of your life. Remember to pay attention to your body and listen to its needs, as this will help you maintain a healthy chakra system.

Heart Chakra Balancing Techniques

The fourth chakra, or the heart chakra, is the center of love, compassion, and empathy. It is the bridge between the lower chakras, which are related to our physical and emotional needs, and the higher chakras, which are related to our spiritual development.

When the heart chakra is in balance, we experience feelings of unconditional love, forgiveness, and peace. However, when it is imbalanced, we may experience feelings of jealousy, anger, or resentment.

Here are some heart chakra balancing techniques that you can try:

1. Practice self-love and self-care. Take time for yourself to do things that bring you joy and happiness, such as taking a bath, going for a walk, or reading a book.

2. Practice forgiveness. Holding onto anger or resentment can block the flow of love in our lives. Try to forgive yourself and others for past mistakes and hurts.

3. Engage in acts of kindness. Doing good deeds for others can open up our hearts and cultivate feelings of compassion and empathy.

4. Connect with nature. Spend time in nature, whether it's going for a hike or simply sitting outside and observing the beauty around you.

5. Practice heart-opening yoga poses. Certain yoga poses, such as camel pose or bridge pose, can help to open up the heart chakra and release any blockages.

Remember, a balanced heart chakra allows us to love ourselves and others unconditionally, fostering positive relationships and a sense of inner peace. By incorporating these heart chakra balancing techniques into your daily routine, you can cultivate a more loving and compassionate outlook on life.

Throat Chakra Balancing Techniques

The Throat Chakra, also called "Vishuddha, is the center of communication and self-expression. An imbalance in this chakra can cause difficulties in expressing oneself, fear of public speaking, and social anxiety. Fortunately, there are many techniques you can use to balance this chakra and promote clear communication.

1. Chanting: One of the simplest ways to balance the Throat Chakra is through chanting. You can chant the mantra "ham" while focusing on your throat area. This will help clear any blockages in the chakra and improve communication.

2. Essential Oils: Using essential oils is another effective way to balance the Throat Chakra. Essential oils like peppermint, eucalyptus, and lavender can help soothe and heal the throat area, promoting better communication.

3. Singing: Singing is a great way to improve communication skills and balance the Throat Chakra. Singing helps to clear any blockages in the chakra and promotes healthy self-expression. You don't need to be a professional singer, just sing in the shower or in the car!

4. Blue Crystal Meditation: Meditating with blue crystals such as Blue Lace Agate, Aquamarine, and Lapis Lazuli can help balance the Throat Chakra. Hold the crystal in your hand and focus on your throat area while taking deep breaths.

5. Throat Chakra Yoga Poses: Practicing yoga poses like the Fish Pose (Matsyasana) and the Shoulder Stand (Sarvangasana) can help balance the Throat Chakra. These poses help stimulate and strengthen the throat area, improving communication and self-expression.

Third Eye Chakra Balancing Techniques

The third eye chakra, also known as the Ajna chakra, is located between the eyebrows and is associated with intuition, wisdom, and inner vision. Imbalanced crown chakra can manifest in confusion, inability to think or focus, or an inability to make decisions.

You can rebalance your third eye chakra using several techniques:

1. Meditation: Regular meditation is a great way to open up your third eye chakra and promote clarity of thought. Simply sit comfortably and focus your attention on the space between your eyebrows, taking deep breaths in and out.

2. Aromatherapy: Essential oils like frankincense, clary sage, and sandalwood can help to stimulate the third eye chakra. Use them in a diffuser, or apply them directly to the forehead.

3. Visualization: Imagining a bright purple light in the area of your third eye can help to open up this chakra. Focus your attention on this area while you visualize this light expanding and radiating throughout your body.

4. Yoga poses: Certain yoga poses, like downward dog and child's pose, can help to stimulate the third eye chakra. Include these poses in your regular yoga practice.

5. Crystals: Amethyst and lapis lazuli are two crystals that are particularly effective for balancing the third eye chakra. Hold them in your hand or place them on your forehead during meditation to enhance their benefits.

By using these techniques to balance your third eye chakra, you can experience greater clarity and intuition in your daily life. Remember that each chakra is interconnected, so it's important to work on balancing all of them for optimal energy flow and overall well-being.

Crown Chakra Balancing Techniques

The crown chakra, also called the sahasrara chakra, is the highest energy center in the body. It is associated with spirituality, divine consciousness, and enlightenment. Disconnection, spiritual crisis, and a sense of purpose are signs of an imbalanced crown chakra.

Here are some techniques to balance your crown chakra:

1. Meditation: The crown chakra is often associated with meditation practices, as it helps to calm the mind and allow for a greater connection to spirituality. Sit comfortably in a quiet place, close your eyes, and focus on your breath. Visualize a bright light above your head, slowly descending and filling your body with divine energy.

2. Practice gratitude: Gratitude is a powerful way to activate the crown chakra. Take a few minutes each day to reflect on all the blessings in your life and give thanks. You can also create a gratitude journal and write down the things you are thankful for.

3. Connect with nature: Spending time in nature can help to open and balance the crown chakra. Go for a walk in the park, sit under a tree, or spend time gardening. Connect with the natural world and allow yourself to feel its energy.

4. Seek guidance from a spiritual teacher or mentor: Sometimes we need guidance to help us connect with our spirituality. Seek out a teacher or mentor who can help you on your journey. They may have wisdom and insight that can help you balance your crown chakra.

By incorporating these techniques into your daily routine, you can help to balance your crown chakra and connect with your higher self. Remember, each chakra is interconnected, and by balancing one, you can help to balance the others as well.

By taking the time to understand and balance your chakra system, you can create a harmonious flow of energy throughout your body, mind, and spirit. Imbalanced chakras can lead to physical and emotional discomfort, while balanced chakras can bring clarity, vitality, and inner peace.

Using various techniques such as meditation, yoga, sound therapy, and energy healing, you can rebalance each chakra and bring your energy system into wholeness. It is important to remember that balancing your chakras is an ongoing practice and requires patience and commitment.

As you work to rebalance your chakras, you may also begin to notice positive changes in your life, including increased energy, better sleep, improved relationships, and greater self-awareness. Remember to listen to your body and trust your intuition as you embark on this journey of self-healing and transformation.

Chapter 10: Living in Alignment: Chakra Maintenance for Everyday Life

Are you looking for a way to achieve daily harmony in your life? Chakra maintenance is a powerful tool that can help you create balance and harmony in your daily life. Chakra care involves understanding and tending to your seven main chakras, or energy centers. This blog post will explore the basics of chakra care and how it can help you live in alignment with your true self. We'll discuss the importance of chakra maintenance and some simple tips and techniques to help you create more balance in your life. By taking a mindful approach to chakra care, you can increase your energy levels and overall well-being.

Understanding the Chakras

Chakras are energy centers in the body that are responsible for various aspects of physical, emotional, and spiritual well-being. There are seven main chakras, starting at the base of the spine and ending at the top of the head.

Each chakra corresponds to a specific color, element, and area of the body, as well as specific emotions, behaviors, and beliefs. For example, the root chakra, located at the base of the spine, is associated with the color red, the element of earth, and the physical body. It is also connected to issues of safety, security, and survival.

The second chakra, located in the pelvic area, is associated with the color orange, the element of water, and creativity and sexuality. The third chakra, located in the solar plexus, is associated with the color yellow, the element of fire, and personal power and confidence.

The fourth chakra, located in the heart, is associated with the color green, the element of air, and love and compassion. The fifth chakra, located in the throat, is associated with the color blue, the element of ether, and communication and self-expression.

The sixth chakra, located in the forehead, is associated with the color indigo, the element of light, and intuition and wisdom. The seventh chakra, located at the top of the head, is associated with the color violet, the element of thought, and spiritual connection and enlightenment.

Understanding the chakras and their correspondences can help you identify areas of imbalance in your life and develop a plan for chakra maintenance. By working to balance and cleanse your chakras, you can achieve greater physical, emotional, and spiritual harmony and live your best life.

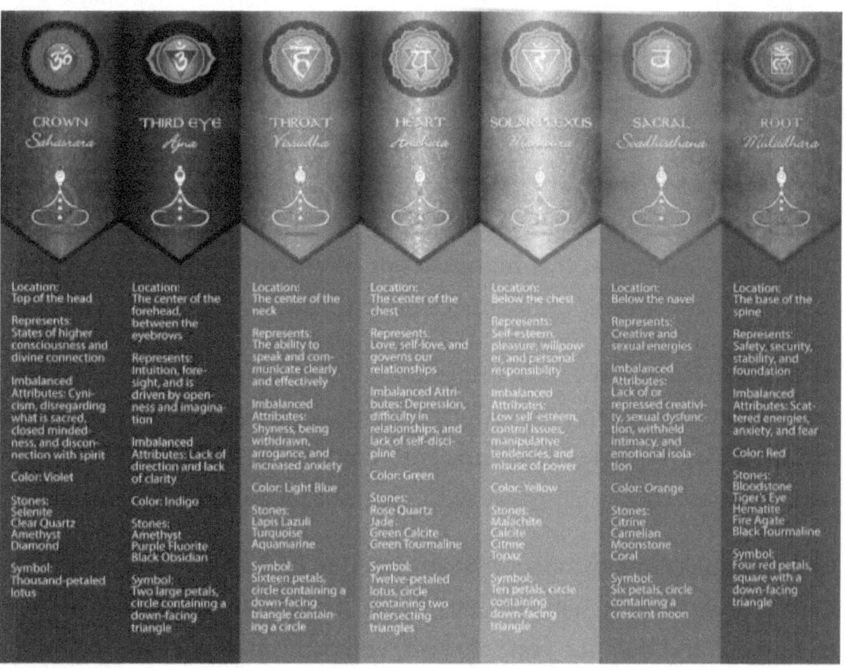

Benefits of Chakra Maintenance

Incorporating chakra maintenance into your daily routine can have numerous benefits for your physical, emotional, and spiritual health. Here are just a few of the benefits of maintaining balanced chakras:

1. Improved Physical Health: When your chakras are balanced and flowing smoothly, your body is better equipped to heal itself and maintain optimal health. Imbalanced chakras, on the other hand, can lead to physical ailments, such as headaches, digestive issues, and fatigue.

2. Increased Emotional Well-Being: The chakras are closely linked to our emotions, and imbalances in our chakras can manifest as emotional difficulties, such as anxiety, depression, and low self-esteem. By maintaining balanced chakras, we can experience greater emotional stability, inner peace, and happiness.

3. Heightened Spiritual Awareness: The chakras are also associated with spiritual development and enlightenment. By keeping our chakras in balance, we can access higher states of consciousness, tap into our intuition, and deepen our connection with the divine.

4. Greater Resilience to Stress: Balanced chakras can help us manage stress more effectively and reduce the impact it has on our bodies and minds. By staying grounded and centered through chakra maintenance, we can handle life's challenges with greater ease and grace.

Overall, chakra maintenance is an essential aspect of self-care and can have far-reaching benefits for every area of your life. By taking the time to nurture and balance your chakras, you can achieve greater harmony and well-being in all aspects of your daily life.

How to Assess Your Chakras

Assessing your chakras is an important step in understanding how they are functioning and identifying any areas that may need attention. There are several ways to assess your chakras, including physical sensations, emotional states, and mental awareness.

One of the easiest ways to assess your chakras is to simply pay attention to how your body feels. Each chakra is associated with specific physical sensations, so tuning into your body can provide valuable information about the state of your chakras. For example, if you feel tension in your stomach or digestive system, it may indicate an imbalance in your solar plexus chakra.

Emotions are another indicator of chakra health. Each chakra is associated with specific emotional states, so noticing your emotional patterns can help you identify which chakras may be blocked or overactive. For instance, if you find yourself feeling anxious or fearful often, it may indicate a blockage in your root or sacral chakra.

Mental awareness is also important in assessing your chakras. Each chakra is associated with different thought patterns, so becoming aware of your thoughts can help identify areas that may need attention. For example, if you find yourself stuck in negative thought patterns or have difficulty expressing yourself, it may indicate an imbalance in your throat chakra.

To assess your chakras, take some time to tune into your body, emotions, and thoughts. Notice any patterns or areas that may need attention and use this information to guide your chakra care routine. With consistent maintenance, you can achieve balance and harmony in your chakras and in turn, your everyday life.

Techniques for Balancing and Cleansing Your

Chakras

Now that you've assessed your chakras and identified any imbalances, it's time to learn how to balance and cleanse them. Here are some techniques to help you achieve harmony and balance in your chakras:

1. Meditation: Meditation is a powerful tool for balancing and cleansing your chakras. Choose a comfortable place to sit, close your eyes, and focus on your breath. As you inhale, imagine that you are breathing in positive energy, and as you exhale, release any negative energy from your body. Visualize a bright light entering each of your chakras, filling them with positive energy and balancing them.

2. Yoga: Practicing yoga can also help to balance and cleanse your chakras. Each yoga pose is designed to target specific chakras, helping to stimulate and balance them. Poses such as the downward-facing dog, cat-cow pose, and warrior pose are great for balancing the root chakra. The fish pose, shoulder stand, and plow pose is beneficial for the throat chakra. The cobra pose, child's pose, and tree pose are helpful for the heart chakra.

3. Chakra Stones: Using chakra stones is another way to balance and cleanse your chakras. Each chakra is associated with a specific stone, such as amethyst for the crown chakra, citrine for the solar plexus chakra, and rose quartz for the heart chakra. Simply place the stone on the corresponding chakra and allow its energy to balance and cleanse the chakra.

4. Essential Oils: Essential oils are another effective way to balance and cleanse your chakras. Each chakra is associated with a specific scent, such as lavender for the crown chakra, peppermint for the throat chakra, and sandalwood for the root chakra. Diffusing the corresponding essential oil or applying it topically can help to balance and cleanse the chakra.

By practicing these techniques regularly, you can achieve balance and harmony in your chakras and maintain optimal physical, mental, and emotional health. Remember that each technique is unique, and what works for one person may not work for another. Experiment with different techniques and find what works best for you.

Incorporating Chakra Care into Your Daily Routine

Taking care of your chakras doesn't have to be a time-consuming task that requires a lot of effort. In fact, there are simple and easy ways to incorporate chakra care into your daily routine. Here are some tips to get you started:

1. Morning meditation: Begin your day by taking a few minutes to meditate and focus on your chakras. Visualize each chakra and imagine a bright, vibrant energy flowing through them.

2. Yoga practice: Incorporating yoga poses that stimulate each chakra is a great way to balance your energy centers. Start with basic poses like Mountain Pose for the root chakra, Tree Pose for the sacral chakra, Warrior II for the solar plexus chakra, Camel Pose for the heart chakra, Shoulder Stand for the throat chakra, Third Eye Pose for the third eye chakra, and Lotus Pose for the crown chakra.

3. Aromatherapy: Certain essential oils have a powerful effect on our chakras. Choose an essential oil that corresponds to the chakra you want to work on, like lavender for the crown chakra or rose for the heart chakra. Use a diffuser or mix the essential oil with a carrier oil and apply it to your pulse points.

4. Mindful eating: Paying attention to the colors and flavors of the food you eat can help activate the chakras. Try to eat a rainbow of fruits and vegetables to stimulate all of your chakras.

5. Daily affirmations: Speak positive affirmations that correspond to each chakra. For example, for the root chakra, you might say, "I am grounded and secure." For the heart chakra, you might say, "I love and accept myself and others unconditionally."

By incorporating these simple practices into your daily routine, you can promote harmony and balance within your chakras. As you become more attuned to your energy centers, you'll be better equipped to navigate life's challenges with ease and grace.

Chakra Maintenance for Specific Situations (e.g. work, relationships, stress)

We all experience various situations in life that can cause imbalances in our chakras. Understanding how to maintain your chakras in these specific situations can help you stay in harmony and achieve optimal well-being. Here are some ways to maintain your chakras in different situations:

- **Focus on the Root Chakra:** Since work is a significant source of stability and security, it is important to maintain the Root Chakra. Try grounding exercises and affirmations that help you feel more secure and stable.

- **Energize your Solar Plexus Chakra:** The Solar Plexus Chakra governs our energy levels, confidence, and self-esteem. If you feel stuck at work or struggle with decision-making, energize your Solar Plexus Chakra by practicing self-love, taking time to do things you enjoy and practicing assertiveness.

- **Open the Heart Chakra:** Relationships can be emotionally challenging, which can cause imbalances in our Heart Chakra. Try opening up your Heart Chakra by practicing self-compassion and empathy towards others.

- **Balance your Throat Chakra:** Communication is key to any successful relationship, so maintaining a healthy Throat Chakra is essential. Practice speaking truthfully and respectfully and be willing to listen to others.

- **Strengthen your Root Chakra:** When we experience stress, our sense of security and stability is often threatened. Strengthen your Root Chakra by practicing grounding exercises and meditations.

- **Calm the Third Eye Chakra:** Stress can make it difficult to focus and cause confusion. Calm your Third Eye Chakra by practicing mindfulness techniques, meditation, and staying in the present moment.

Incorporating these chakra maintenance techniques into your daily routine can help you stay in harmony, no matter what situations you encounter. Remember to take time to assess your chakras regularly and practice self-care to keep them in balance. Additionally, it's important to recognize when you're experiencing common chakra blocks and know how to overcome them. Some common chakra blocks include fear, self-doubt, and past trauma. Overcoming these blocks requires a deep understanding of your inner self and often involves practices like meditation, therapy, and energy healing.

Finally, combining chakra care with other self-care practices can help you achieve optimal well-being. Practices like yoga, acupuncture, and massage can help release energy blockages and promote balance throughout the body. Additionally, a healthy diet, regular exercise, and getting enough sleep can also support the overall health of your chakras.

Incorporating chakra care into your daily routine can seem overwhelming at first, but with time and practice, it will become a natural part of your self-care routine. Remember to be patient with yourself and listen to your body's needs. By taking care of your chakras, you can achieve daily harmony and live your life to its fullest potential.

Common Chakra Blocks and How to Overcome Them

Chakra blocks can occur for many reasons, including physical, emotional, and mental imbalances. They can manifest in different ways, such as physical pain, negative emotions, and overall feelings of being stuck. However, recognizing and overcoming these blocks can help us move toward greater alignment and balance.

Here are some common chakra blocks and tips on how to overcome them:

Root Chakra Block:

A block in the root chakra can lead to feelings of anxiety, insecurity, and a lack of groundedness. This can be caused by a lack of physical activity, a disconnection from nature, or feelings of instability in our living situations.

How to overcome it:

Incorporating physical exercise, such as yoga or hiking, can help to ground and stabilize the root chakra. Spending time in nature and reconnecting with the earth can also be helpful, as well as establishing a sense of security and stability in our living arrangements.

Sacral Chakra Block:

A block in the sacral chakra can result in creative blocks, lack of passion or motivation, and emotional imbalances. This can be caused by a lack of creative expression, repressed emotions, or unhealthy relationships.

How to overcome it:

Allowing for creative expressions, such as painting or dancing, can help to activate the sacral chakra. Taking time to acknowledge and process our emotions, perhaps through therapy or journaling, can also be helpful. Setting boundaries and creating healthy relationships can also help to support the sacral chakra.

Solar Plexus Chakra Block:

A block in the solar plexus chakra can lead to low self-esteem, feelings of powerlessness, and a lack of confidence. This can be caused by a lack of control or direction in our lives, negative self-talk, or past trauma.

How to overcome it:

Working towards establishing a sense of control and direction in our lives, such as through goal setting or creating a daily routine, can help to activate the solar plexus chakra. Changing negative self-talk to positive affirmations and seeking therapy to process past traumas can also be beneficial.

These are just a few examples of common chakra blocks and ways to overcome them. By taking time to assess and work towards balancing and cleansing our chakras, we can move towards greater harmony and alignment in our everyday lives.

Combining Chakra Care with Other Self-Care Practices

Maintaining the health and harmony of your chakras is an essential aspect of self-care, but it doesn't have to be the only one. In fact, you can combine your chakra care routine with other self-care practices to enhance your overall well-being.

For instance, practicing yoga is an excellent way to balance and stimulate your chakras while also benefiting your physical health. There are numerous yoga poses and sequences that focus on different chakras, and by incorporating them into your practice, you can improve both your physical and energetic health.

Meditation is another powerful self-care practice that complements chakra care. By quieting your mind and focusing on your breath, you can become more aware of your chakras and the energy flowing through them. You can also use guided meditations that focus on chakra balancing to enhance the effects of your chakra care practice.

Eating a healthy and balanced diet is another crucial component of self-care that can support your chakra health. Each chakra is associated with different foods, so incorporating a variety of fruits, vegetables, nuts, and whole grains into your diet can help balance and support your chakras.

Finally, getting enough sleep and rest is essential for overall health and well-being, including your chakra health. During sleep, your body repairs and rejuvenates itself, including your chakras. Aim to get at least seven to eight hours of quality sleep each night to support your chakra care routine.

Incorporating chakra care into your other self-care practices can enhance their effects and support your overall well-being. Remember that self-care is not a one-size-fits-all approach, so experiment with different practices and techniques to find what works best for you. In addition to yoga, meditation, a healthy diet, and sleep, there are other self-care practices that can complement your chakra care routine. For example, spending time in nature can help ground and balance your root chakra, while practicing gratitude can support your heart chakra.

Journaling is another useful tool for chakra care, as it allows you to explore and reflect on your thoughts and emotions. You can use journal prompts that focus on each chakra to gain insight and clarity into areas of your life that may need attention or healing.

If you find that your chakras are consistently imbalanced or blocked, consider seeking out additional support from a qualified practitioner. This could include energy healing sessions, acupuncture, or other holistic modalities that focus on chakra health and balance.

Remember that self-care and chakra care are ongoing practices, and it's important to make them a part of your daily routine. By taking care of your chakras, you can support your physical, emotional, and spiritual health and live in greater harmony and balance.

Chapter 11: Chakras and Relationships: Cultivating Connection and Harmony

Chakras: The Key to Understanding and Improving Your Relationships

Are you struggling to understand and improve your relationships? If so, the answer may lie in an ancient Eastern philosophy known as chakras. Chakras are energy centers located within the body that are believed to be connected to the flow of energy that affects physical, mental, and spiritual well-being. By learning about and exploring the chakras, you can gain insight into your relationships and gain the tools you need to cultivate connection and harmony. In this chapter, we'll explore how chakras can help you better understand and improve your relationships.

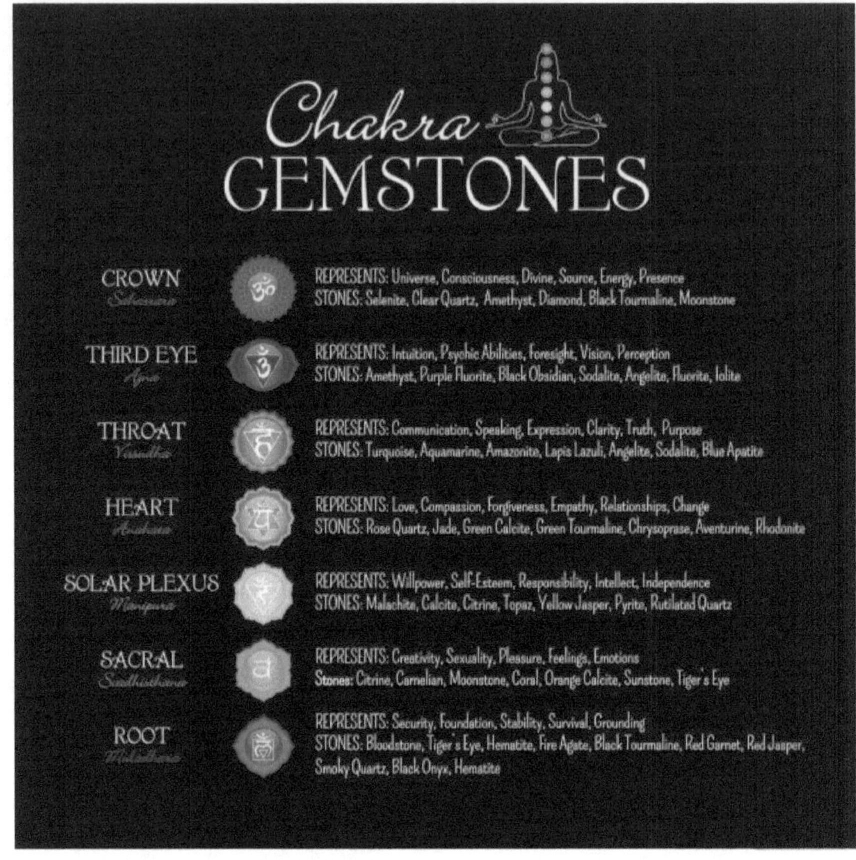

Understanding Chakras and Their Role in Relationships

Chakras are energetic centers within the body that help regulate the flow of energy. When these centers are balanced, it leads to an overall sense of well-being and vitality. When they are out of balance, however, it can lead to emotional, physical, and mental issues.

Our chakras play an essential role in our relationships. They impact the way we interact with others, the way we express ourselves, and how we handle conflicts. By understanding the role of chakras in relationships, we can cultivate deeper connections and harmony with our loved ones.

There are seven main chakras in the body, each associated with different aspects of our physical, emotional, and spiritual health. By focusing on each of these chakras and bringing them into balance, we can improve our relationships and overall well-being.

In the following sections, we will explore the role of each chakra in relationships and how we can work to balance them. From building a strong foundation for relationships to developing personal power and authenticity, understanding the chakras is key to unlocking deeper and more fulfilling relationships.

Root Chakra: Building a Strong Foundation for Relationships

The Root Chakra is the foundation of all chakras and is associated with our basic needs and survival instincts. This chakra is responsible for our sense of security, safety, and stability in life, which are essential for healthy relationships. When the Root Chakra is balanced, we feel grounded and confident in ourselves and can develop healthy connections with others.

Building a strong foundation for relationships starts with grounding ourselves. This can be achieved through physical activity, such as walking or yoga, spending time in nature, or even just focusing on our breath and connecting with the present moment. When we ground ourselves, we are better able to show up in our relationships, communicate effectively, and make wise decisions.

Additionally, the Root Chakra is also associated with our family of origin and childhood experiences. If we have unresolved issues or trauma related to our family or childhood, it can manifest in our current relationships. Taking time to work through these past experiences can help us to establish healthy patterns and develop stronger connections with others.

In order to strengthen our Root Chakra, it's important to focus on self-care and establishing healthy boundaries. We can do this by taking time to prioritize our physical and emotional well-being, setting clear boundaries with others, and learning to say no when necessary.

Overall, by building a strong foundation with our Root Chakra, we can establish a sense of security and stability in our relationships, allowing us to cultivate deeper connections with others.

Sacral Chakra: Enhancing Emotional Intimacy and Sensuality

The sacral chakra is located just below the navel, and it is associated with the emotional and sexual aspects of our relationships. When this chakra is balanced, we are able to connect deeply with our partners and express ourselves freely.

One way to enhance the sacral chakra is to prioritize physical touch and intimacy in our relationships. This could mean making time for regular date nights, cuddling, and exploring new ways of experiencing pleasure together.

Another way to enhance the sacral chakra is to cultivate emotional intimacy through communication and vulnerability. Sharing our fears, desires, and vulnerabilities with our partners can create a deeper connection and build trust in the relationship.

It's important to note that the sacral chakra can also become imbalanced, leading to issues with emotional intimacy and sexuality in our relationships. For example, an overactive sacral chakra may lead to addictive behaviors or an inability to form lasting connections, while an underactive sacral chakra may lead to disconnection or a lack of sexual desire.

If you feel that your sacral chakra is imbalanced, try incorporating practices such as meditation, yoga, or energy healing to restore balance and enhance emotional intimacy and sensuality in your relationships.

Solar Plexus Chakra: Developing Confidence and Personal Power in Relationships

The third chakra, the solar plexus chakra, is located in the upper abdomen and is associated with personal power, self-confidence, and willpower. This chakra plays a significant role in our relationships as it influences our ability to stand up for ourselves, assert our needs, and express our opinions.

In relationships, it is essential to develop confidence and personal power to avoid being taken advantage of or becoming a people-pleaser. By balancing and activating the solar plexus chakra, we can strengthen our ability to set boundaries, communicate our needs effectively, and stand up for ourselves without being aggressive or defensive.

Here are some practices that can help you develop your solar plexus chakra in relationships:

1. Speak your truth: Honesty and authenticity are vital components of any healthy relationship. Expressing yourself truthfully and assertively can help you build trust and respect with your partner. Make sure to communicate in a way that is respectful and compassionate towards others while also honoring your needs and feelings.

2. Set boundaries: Boundaries are an essential part of developing personal power and self-confidence. When you set boundaries, you are communicating your needs and values and protecting your emotional and physical space. Make sure your boundaries are clear and communicate them assertively but with respect.

3. Trust your gut: The solar plexus chakra is associated with intuition and gut feelings. Trusting your instincts can help you make better decisions in relationships and avoid getting involved in toxic or unhealthy relationships.

4. Embrace your strengths: The solar plexus chakra is associated with personal power, which means you need to embrace your strengths and be confident in your abilities. Acknowledge your talents, skills, and achievements and let them inspire you to take positive action towards building a better relationship.

By working on your solar plexus chakra, you can develop the confidence and personal power necessary for healthy and fulfilling relationships. Remember that balance and activation of all the chakras are necessary for overall harmony in your relationships. So keep working on yourself and watch as your relationships start to flourish.

Heart Chakra: Cultivating Love, Compassion, and Forgiveness in Relationships

The Heart Chakra, also known as Anahata in Sanskrit, is located at the center of the chest and is associated with love, compassion, and forgiveness. When this chakra is balanced and open, it allows us to connect deeply with ourselves and others, creating a sense of warmth, empathy, and harmony.

In relationships, the Heart Chakra is a vital component for creating a loving and compassionate connection. It allows us to see others as they truly are, accept them without judgment, and respond with kindness and understanding. It also enables us to forgive ourselves and others for past hurts, leading to healing and growth.

To cultivate a healthy Heart Chakra in your relationships, consider the following practices:

1. Practice self-love: Take time to nurture and care for yourself. Listen to your needs and desires and honor them without judgment. Treat yourself with kindness, respect, and compassion.

2. Cultivate empathy: Put yourself in others' shoes and try to understand their perspectives. Listen deeply and communicate your understanding. Show compassion for their experiences, feelings, and needs.

3. Practice forgiveness: Let go of resentments and grudges that may be blocking your heart. Release negative emotions and practice forgiveness for yourself and others.

4. Show gratitude: Express appreciation and thankfulness for the positive qualities and experiences in your life. Focus on what you do have, rather than what you lack.

By cultivating love, compassion, and forgiveness in your Heart Chakra, you can create a healthy and loving foundation for your relationships. Remember, the key to healthy relationships starts with a healthy relationship with yourself. Practice self-love, cultivate empathy, and show forgiveness and gratitude, and watch your relationships flourish.

Throat Chakra: Practicing Communication and Authenticity in Relationships

Vishuddha is the Sanskrit word for throat, so throat chakra would be located in the neck. This chakra is associated with communication, self-expression, and authenticity. It governs the throat, mouth, neck, and thyroid gland.

In relationships, the throat chakra plays a vital role in how we communicate with our partners. When the throat chakra is balanced, we can express ourselves authentically and communicate our needs effectively. This leads to healthy and fulfilling relationships.

However, when the throat chakra is blocked or imbalanced, we may struggle to express ourselves, leading to misunderstandings and conflicts. It can also lead to us holding back our true thoughts and feelings, which can hinder intimacy and connection.

To balance and open the throat chakra in relationships, practicing authentic communication is essential. This means being honest and clear about what we want and need from our partner, while also listening actively and with empathy to their needs and desires.

It also means expressing ourselves in a way that is true to who we are, without fear of judgment or rejection. This requires us to be vulnerable and open with our partners, sharing our deepest thoughts and feelings with them.

In addition, engaging in creative and expressive activities such as singing, writing, or art can also help to open and balance the throat chakra, allowing us to communicate with more ease and authenticity in our relationships.

Ultimately, by practicing authentic communication and opening our throat chakra, we can cultivate deeper connections and greater harmony in our relationships, leading to more fulfilling and joyful experiences with our loved ones.

Third Eye Chakra: Trusting Your Intuition and

Wisdom in Relationships

The third eye chakra, located in the center of the forehead, is associated with intuition and wisdom. When this chakra is balanced, we can tap into our inner guidance system and make decisions that align with our deepest values and desires. This is particularly important in relationships, where our emotions can sometimes cloud our judgment and lead us astray.

Trusting our intuition and wisdom in relationships means listening to our inner voice and paying attention to the signs and signals that come our way. It also means being open to learning and growing, even when things don't go as planned.

One way to strengthen the third eye chakra is through meditation and visualization. You can imagine a bright indigo light filling your forehead and opening your intuition and insight. You can also practice paying attention to your dreams and journaling about your inner guidance.

In relationships, trusting your intuition and wisdom means being true to yourself and not compromising your values or beliefs. It means setting healthy boundaries and speaking up when something doesn't feel right. It also means being patient and trusting that the universe has a plan, even if it's not always clear in the moment.

Ultimately, the third eye chakra reminds us that we have the power to create the relationships we desire, by tapping into our intuition and wisdom and trusting the path that unfolds. When we trust ourselves, we can build deeper and more fulfilling connections with others, based on mutual respect, honesty, and authenticity.

Crown Chakra: Finding Connection and Transcendence in Relationships

The crown chakra is the highest chakra and represents our connection to the divine and our spiritual nature. It is located at the top of the head and is associated with the color purple or white. This chakra is all about transcendence and going beyond our physical existence.

In relationships, the crown chakra can help us find a deeper level of connection with our partner and the universe as a whole. It can help us see the bigger picture and understand that our relationship is just one small piece in the grand scheme of things.

To activate and balance your crown chakra in your relationships, try these practices:

1. Meditation: Spend time in meditation each day to quiet your mind and connect with your higher self. This can help you find clarity and guidance in your relationships.

2. Gratitude: Practice gratitude daily by reflecting on all the things in your life that you are thankful for, including your relationship. This can help you see the positive aspects of your partnership and appreciate your connection with your partner.

3. Surrender: Learn to surrender control and trust in the universe. This can help you let go of any worries or fears you may have about your relationship and allow things to flow naturally.

4. Service: Find ways to serve others and make a positive impact in the world. This can help you feel more connected to humanity as a whole and inspire you to be a better partner in your relationship.

By activating and balancing your crown chakra, you can find a deeper sense of connection and transcendence in your relationships. You may begin to see your partner and your relationship in a new light, with a deeper understanding of your place in the universe.

Chapter 12: Chakras and Consciousness: Expanding Our Spiritual Connection

Our spiritual connection is an important part of our overall well-being. In this chapter we will explore the concepts of chakras and consciousness, and how they can help us expand our spiritual connection. The ancient practice of energy healing, known as chakra balancing, works to align and open the body's seven main energy centers, which are also known as chakras. Through the practice of conscious awareness and meditation, we can learn how to unlock the power of these energy centers and use them to deepen our spiritual connection and open a world of possibilities.

Understanding Chakras

Chakras, also known as energy centers, are believed to be a fundamental aspect of the human experience and the spiritual world. They are an essential part of many spiritual traditions, including Hinduism, Buddhism, and Yoga. Chakras are said to be centers of energy in the body that correspond to different aspects of human life and consciousness. There are seven major chakras, each with its own distinct qualities, characteristics, and meaning.

According to traditional Indian teachings, chakras are located along the spinal column and represent the physical, emotional, and spiritual aspects of our being. Each chakra is believed to be responsible for specific physiological functions and related emotional and spiritual states.

The concept of chakras is based on the idea that the body contains subtle energy, often called prana or life force, which flows through specific channels, or nadis, that run throughout the body. These nadis intersect at different points, forming the chakras.

Understanding the chakras is an important part of many spiritual practices, as they can be used to identify areas of imbalance and guide healing and self-improvement. Through balancing and harmonizing the chakras, practitioners can achieve greater physical health, emotional stability, and spiritual connection.

In the following sections, we will explore the seven chakras and their meanings, as well as practical ways to balance and work with these energy centers to promote well-being and expand our spiritual connection.

The Seven Chakras and Their Meanings

We have seven chakras in our bodies that regulate our physical, emotional, and spiritual well-being. Each chakra has a unique color and represents different aspects of our lives. Understanding these chakras and their meanings can help us connect with our bodies and become more in tune with our spiritual selves.

The Root Chakra, located at the base of the spine, is associated with grounding, survival, and our connection to the physical world. The color associated with this chakra is red.

The Sacral Chakra, located just below the belly button, is associated with creativity, sexuality, and pleasure. The color associated with this chakra is orange.

The Solar Plexus Chakra, located in the stomach area, is associated with personal power, self-esteem, and confidence. The color associated with this chakra is yellow.

The Heart Chakra, this chakra, located in the chest, is linked with love, compassion, and connection. The color associated with this chakra is green.

The Throat Chakra, located in the throat area, is associated with communication, self-expression, and speaking your truth. The color associated with this chakra is blue.

The Third Eye Chakra, located between the eyebrows, is associated with intuition, perception, and wisdom. The color associated with this chakra is indigo.

The Crown Chakra, located at the top of the head, is associated with spiritual connection, higher consciousness, and enlightenment. The color associated with this chakra is violet or white.

Understanding the meanings and associations of each chakra can help us identify where we may have imbalances in our lives. By balancing and clearing these chakras, we can improve our overall health and well-being and become more connected to our spiritual selves.

Balancing Your Chakras for Improved Health and Wellbeing

The seven chakras are interconnected energy centers in the body. Each is associated with different aspects of our physical, emotional, and spiritual well-being. When these energy centers become blocked or unbalanced, it can lead to a range of physical and emotional symptoms. However, by practicing techniques to balance our chakras, we can improve our overall health and well-being.

One way to balance your chakras is through the practice of yoga. Certain yoga poses can help activate and balance specific chakras within the body. For example, the Root Chakra is associated with grounding and stability, so practicing standing poses like Tree Pose or Warrior II can help activate this energy center.

Another way to balance your chakras is through the use of crystals and gemstones. Each chakra is associated with specific stones that can help balance and activate that particular energy center. For example, the Heart Chakra is associated with the rose quartz crystal, which is said to promote love, compassion, and forgiveness.

Meditation is another effective technique for balancing your chakras. By focusing your attention on each chakra and visualizing it spinning and radiating energy, you can help activate and balance these energy centers within your body. There are also guided chakra meditation practices available that can help you deepen your connection to your chakras.

Finally, it's important to pay attention to your body and your emotions. If you're experiencing physical or emotional symptoms that correspond to a specific chakra, this may be an indication that that energy center is blocked or unbalanced. By being mindful of your body and emotions, you can become more aware of areas that need attention and take steps to balance your chakras.

Overall, balancing your chakras can have a profound impact on your physical, emotional, and spiritual well-being. By practicing techniques to activate and balance these energy centers within your body, you can improve your overall health and cultivate a deeper connection to your spiritual self.

Expanding Consciousness Through Chakra Meditation

Meditation has been used for centuries to promote relaxation and inner peace. It's also a powerful tool for expanding our consciousness and connecting with our spiritual selves. By focusing on our chakras during meditation, we can tap into a higher level of awareness and access the energy centers within our bodies.

Chakra meditation involves visualizing each of the seven chakras and their corresponding colors. Start at the base of the spine and work your way up, spending a few minutes on each chakra. As you visualize the chakra, focus on breathing in positive energy and releasing any negativity or blockages.

As you move through each chakra, you may notice sensations in your body. These could include warmth, tingling, or a sense of release. Don't worry if you don't feel anything at first; it takes time and practice to tune into the subtle energies of the chakras.

By regularly practicing chakra meditation, you can increase your awareness of your own energy and develop a deeper connection with your spiritual self. It can also help you release negative emotions and promote healing on a physical and emotional level.

Incorporating chakra meditation into your daily routine doesn't have to be complicated or time-consuming. Even just a few minutes each day can make a big difference in how you feel. Consider starting your day with a quick chakra meditation to set a positive tone for the rest of your day.

If you're new to chakra meditation, there are plenty of guided meditations available online or through apps that can help you get started. As you become more comfortable with the practice, you may choose to experiment with different techniques and incorporate other aspects of chakra healing into your spiritual practice.

Chakra Healing Techniques for Deep Emotional Release

As we've discussed earlier, our chakras are centers of energy that help us maintain physical, emotional, and spiritual balance. However, when these energy centers become blocked, it can cause disruptions in our lives. This can lead to negative emotions, physical discomfort, and even illness.

Fortunately, there are many ways to clear blockages and promote healing within the chakras. One effective technique is to focus on chakra healing for deep emotional release. This approach involves using specific methods to clear out the negative emotions and traumas that have been stored within our energy centers.

Here are some chakra healing techniques that can help you achieve deep emotional release:

1. Visualization: Visualization is a powerful technique that involves creating mental images to promote healing. You can imagine your chakras as bright, glowing spheres of light. Picture them filling with positive energy, expanding and flowing freely throughout your body. This can help clear blockages and promote emotional release.

2. Sound Therapy: Sound therapy is a popular form of chakra healing that involves using specific frequencies and vibrations to promote healing within the energy centers. This can include listening to music that resonates with the frequency of a particular chakra or using singing bowls, gongs, or tuning forks to promote vibrational healing.

3. Affirmations: Affirmations are positive statements that you repeat to yourself to promote healing and positive change. You can use affirmations to target specific chakras and help release emotional blockages. For example, you can repeat affirmations such as "I trust in my intuition" to promote healing within the third eye chakra.

4. Movement and Exercise: Physical movement and exercise can help promote chakra healing by increasing the flow of energy throughout the body. Yoga, for example, is a great way to promote physical and emotional balance while also focusing on specific chakras.

By incorporating these techniques into your chakra healing practice, you can begin to release the negative emotions and traumas that have been stored within your energy centers. This can lead to improved emotional health, physical well-being, and overall spiritual connection.

Incorporating Chakras into Your Spiritual Practice

If you're looking to enhance your spiritual connection, incorporating chakras into your spiritual practice is an excellent way to achieve this. Understanding the energy centers within your body and how they affect your physical, mental, and emotional states can help you to cultivate greater harmony and balance in your life.

To begin incorporating chakras into your spiritual practice, start by becoming familiar with the seven main chakras and their meanings. Each chakra corresponds to a specific area of the body and has a unique function and purpose. By learning about the chakras, you can start to recognize patterns in your own physical, emotional, and mental states and determine which areas of your life could benefit from extra attention.

Once you've gained a basic understanding of the chakras, you can start working on balancing them through various techniques, including chakra meditation and visualization. Regular chakra meditation can help you to focus your awareness on each energy center, bringing greater harmony and balance to your mind and body.

Another way to incorporate chakras into your spiritual practice is through chakra healing techniques. These techniques are designed to help you release emotional blockages and negative energy that may be preventing you from fully connecting with your higher self. Some examples of chakra healing techniques include reiki, acupuncture, and crystal healing.

Finally, consider integrating chakras into your daily life through simple practices such as yoga or mindfulness meditation. By focusing on your breath and aligning your body and mind, you can activate your chakras and achieve a greater sense of balance and inner peace.

Overall, incorporating chakras into your spiritual practice can help you to deepen your connection with yourself and the universe around you. Whether you're new to spirituality or have been practicing for years, exploring the world of chakras can be an exciting and rewarding journey.

Incorporating chakras into your spiritual practice can also involve creating a sacred space or altar where you can focus on your connection to the energy centers in your body. You might include items that represent each chakra, such as crystals or colored candles, and spend time each day in meditation or reflection.

Another way to deepen your spiritual connection with your chakras is to practice gratitude and affirmations. By acknowledging and appreciating the positive aspects of your life, you can activate the higher-frequency vibrations associated with each chakra. For example, focusing on gratitude for your physical body can help activate the root chakra, while gratitude for creativity and expression can activate the sacral chakra.

Incorporating chakras into your spiritual practice can be a transformative journey that allows you to expand your consciousness and achieve a greater sense of purpose and fulfillment. Whether you're just starting out or are a seasoned spiritual practitioner, exploring the world of chakras can offer valuable insights and tools for improving your physical, emotional, and spiritual well-being. By working to balance and align your chakras, you can cultivate a deeper sense of inner peace and harmony and connect more fully with the universe around you.

Chapter 13: Chakras in Daily Life: Embodying Balance and Fulfillment

Chakras in Daily Life: Embodying Balance and Fulfillment

Chakras are energy centers in the body that can profoundly influence our physical, emotional, and spiritual health. If these centers become unbalanced, we can experience a range of physical and emotional symptoms. Learning how to work with the chakras on a daily basis can help us to cultivate balance and fulfillment in our lives. In this blog post, we'll explore the seven main chakras and how we can use them to bring greater balance and harmony into our lives.

Understanding Chakras

Chakras are energy centers within the body that are believed to correspond to various physical, emotional, and spiritual functions. In Sanskrit, the word "chakra" translates to "wheel" or "disk" which refers to the circular shape of these energy centers.

There are seven main chakras located along the spine, each representing a different aspect of our being. The first chakra, located at the base of the spine, is associated with our physical body and survival needs. The second chakra, located in the lower abdomen, is linked to our emotions and creativity. The third chakra, located at the solar plexus, relates to our personal power and self-esteem. The fourth chakra, located at the heart, governs our ability to give and receive love. The fifth chakra, located at the throat, is associated with our communication and expression. The sixth chakra, located at the third eye, is linked to our intuition and spiritual awareness. The seventh and final chakra, located at the crown of the head, represents our connection to the divine.

Understanding the function of each chakra is important in maintaining balance and well-being. When one or more chakras are blocked or out of balance, it can lead to physical or emotional problems. Therefore, it is important to regularly check in with our chakras and work to keep them balanced. In doing so, we can cultivate a deeper connection with our higher self and ultimately lead a more fulfilling life.

Importance of Balancing Chakras for Well-being

Chakras are energy centers in the body that influence our physical, emotional, and spiritual well-being. When our chakras are in balance, we experience optimal health and a sense of wholeness. However, when our chakras are blocked or unbalanced, we may experience physical or emotional ailments, feel stuck or unfulfilled in life, and struggle to connect with our higher self.

Balancing our chakras is important for overall well-being, as it helps to release any blockages or excess energy and allows our life force energy to flow freely. This can help to alleviate physical and emotional symptoms, improve mental clarity and focus, and promote a sense of inner peace and calm.

When our chakras are balanced, we are better able to connect with ourselves and the world around us. We may feel more present in our relationships, more creative in our work, and more aligned with our purpose and passions.

By taking the time to balance our chakras regularly, we are investing in our overall well-being and allowing ourselves to live our fullest, most fulfilling lives. So take some time to explore and understand your chakras, and practice balancing them regularly for optimal health and happiness.

One way to balance our chakras is through simple practices like meditation, yoga, or breathwork. These practices can help to bring awareness to the energy centers in our body and allow us to release any blockages or tension that may be preventing us from experiencing balance and harmony.

Incorporating chakra balancing practices into our daily routine can also help to make it a natural part of our life, rather than something we have to set aside time for. This can include things like eating foods that correspond to each chakra, using essential oils or crystals to balance energy, or practicing mindful movement that targets specific chakras.

Ultimately, chakra balancing is not just about physical health, but also about spiritual growth and connecting with our higher self. When we can align our energy centers and connect with our inner truth, we can live a life that is authentic and fulfilling.

So take the time to explore your chakras and find practices that work for you. Whether it's through meditation, yoga, or other forms of self-care, committing to balancing your chakras can help you to embody balance and fulfillment in all aspects of your life.

Simple Practices to Balance Your Chakras

If you're interested in chakra balancing, there are a number of simple practices you can try to help you get started. These practices don't require any special equipment or prior knowledge, and they can be done from the comfort of your own home.

1. Chakra Meditation: One of the simplest ways to balance your chakras is through meditation. Find a quiet and comfortable place to sit and close your eyes. Focus on your breath, and then visualize each chakra in turn, imagining that each one is glowing with its own unique color.

2. Yoga Poses: Certain yoga poses are known to be particularly beneficial for balancing the chakras. For example, the root chakra can be stimulated through poses such as the standing forward bend, while the throat chakra can be stimulated through the fish pose.

3. Essential Oils: Different essential oils are believed to have different effects on the chakras. For example, lavender oil is thought to be helpful for balancing the crown chakra, while lemon oil may be useful for the solar plexus chakra. Experiment with different oils to find what works best for you.

4. Sound Healing: Certain sounds, such as singing bowls, chimes, and gongs, are believed to be beneficial for balancing the chakras. You can purchase your own sound healing instruments, or find videos or guided meditations that incorporate sound healing.

5. Visualization: Visualization exercises can also be helpful for balancing the chakras. For example, you might imagine a beam of white light flowing through each of your chakras, cleansing and balancing them as it goes.

These are just a few of the simple practices you can try to balance your chakras. Remember, it's important to listen to your body and go at your own pace. With time and practice, you may begin to notice positive changes in your overall well-being and sense of fulfillment.

Incorporating Chakra Balancing in Daily Life

Chakra balancing is not just a one-time activity, it is an ongoing process that requires regular attention. In order to maintain balance and harmony in your energy centers, it is important to incorporate chakra-balancing practices into your daily routine. Here are a few simple ways to do this:

1. Meditation: Take out some time every day to meditate and focus on your chakras. You can start by sitting in a comfortable position, closing your eyes, and focusing on your breath. Visualize the energy flowing through each of your chakras, starting from the root and moving up to the crown. This will help you identify any blockages or imbalances and allow you to release them.

2. Yoga: Practicing yoga can also help you balance your chakras. Each yoga pose focuses on a specific chakra, allowing the energy to flow freely through it. For example, the tree pose helps balance the root chakra, while the bridge pose focuses on the heart chakra.

3. Affirmations: Using affirmations can also help you balance your chakras. These are positive statements that can be repeated to yourself to create a positive shift in your thoughts and emotions. You can choose affirmations that correspond to each chakra, such as "I am safe and secure" for the root chakra and "I trust the universe to guide me" for the third eye chakra.

4. Diet: Eating a balanced diet can also help balance your chakras. Each chakra corresponds to specific foods, so including them in your diet can help activate and balance the energy centers. For example, root vegetables like potatoes and carrots can help balance the root chakra, while fruits like berries and grapes can help balance the crown chakra.

Incorporating these practices into your daily routine can help you maintain balance and harmony in your energy centers, leading to a healthier and more fulfilling life.

Connecting with Higher Self through Chakras

Our chakras not only have a direct impact on our physical and emotional health but also provide a path for connecting with our higher selves. Our higher self is our true essence and spiritual connection that exists beyond our ego and limiting beliefs. By balancing our chakras, we create an opportunity to connect with our higher self, align with our true purpose, and experience a greater sense of inner peace and fulfillment.

To connect with your higher self through your chakras, start by focusing on your crown chakra, which is located at the top of your head and represents your spiritual connection. Sit in a comfortable position, close your eyes, and visualize a beam of white light radiating down from the top of your head, through your crown chakra, and down through the rest of your body.

As you continue to focus on your crown chakra, feel the light filling your entire being and illuminating every part of you. Imagine that this light is connecting you to your higher self, and feel the presence of your true essence and inner wisdom. Spend a few moments in this space, allowing yourself to connect with your higher self and receive any insights or guidance that may come.

This simple practice can be incorporated into your daily routine, allowing you to stay connected with your higher self and live a more fulfilling life. By balancing your chakras and connecting with your higher self, you can tap into your true potential and experience a deeper sense of joy, love, and purpose.

Achieving Fulfillment through Chakra Balancing

Balancing your chakras not only enhances your well-being, but it also helps you achieve fulfillment in life. When your chakras are in balance, you can experience a sense of purpose, meaning, and joy.

The lower chakras (root, sacral, and solar plexus) govern our basic needs and desires, such as survival, creativity, and self-confidence. By balancing these chakras, we can feel more grounded, creative, and self-assured. This helps us to pursue our goals with enthusiasm and clarity, leading to a greater sense of fulfillment in life.

The upper chakras (throat, third eye, and crown) govern our spiritual connection, intuition, and wisdom. By balancing these chakras, we can tap into our inner guidance and align with our higher purpose. This leads to a sense of spiritual fulfillment and connection to something greater than us.

Through chakra balancing, we can integrate our physical, emotional, mental, and spiritual aspects, creating a sense of wholeness and fulfillment. By aligning with our true selves and living in harmony with our surroundings, we can experience a fulfilling life.

Chakra balancing can help us identify areas of our lives that may need attention and allow us to address them from a place of balance and inner wisdom. We can cultivate a deeper understanding of our own needs and desires and make choices that support our growth and fulfillment.

Practices such as yoga, meditation, and breathwork can help us balance our chakras and achieve a greater sense of fulfillment in life. By incorporating chakra balancing into our daily routines, we can cultivate a sense of balance, inner peace, and fulfillment.

When we live in alignment with our chakras, we can experience a sense of flow and ease in our lives. We can trust our inner guidance, make decisions with clarity, and move forward with confidence and purpose.

Chakra balancing is not a one-time fix but an ongoing process that requires patience, practice, and self-awareness. By regularly balancing our chakras, we can embody a sense of balance and fulfillment that permeates every aspect of our lives.

Chapter 14: Chakras and the Sacred: Deepening the Spiritual Connection

The concept of chakras is one that has been explored by various spiritual and religious traditions for centuries. In fact, these energy centers are believed to be the source of our physical, mental, and spiritual well-being. Understanding how the chakras work and how to use them to deepen your spiritual connection can be a powerful tool for personal growth and transformation. In this chapter, we will explore the connection between chakras and the sacred, and how it can help us to build a deeper, more meaningful connection with ourselves and the world around us.

Creating Sacred Spaces

To deepen your spiritual connection, it's important to create a sacred space in your home or wherever you feel most comfortable. A sacred space can be any place that you dedicate to your spiritual practice, where you can find peace and tranquility and feel more connected to the divine. This could be a corner of your bedroom, a meditation room, or even a quiet spot outside in nature.

To create a sacred space, you should start by choosing a spot that feels meaningful to you. Once you've found your spot, start decorating it with items that bring you joy and that represent your spirituality. This could be candles, crystals, statues, or any other items that resonate with you.

You can also incorporate elements from nature into your sacred space, such as plants or natural stones. This will help to connect you to the earth and to feel grounded during your spiritual practice.

Finally, consider incorporating a personal altar into your sacred space. This can be a small table or shelf where you can place objects that hold significance for you. This could include photos of loved ones, mementos from important moments in your life, or symbols of your faith or spirituality.

By creating a sacred space, you will have a dedicated place where you can connect with the divine and deepen your spiritual practice.

Sacred Rituals: Meditation, Prayer, Chanting, and Energy Healing

One way to deepen our spiritual connection is by incorporating sacred rituals into our daily practice. Meditation, prayer, chanting, and energy healing are all powerful ways to connect with the divine and create a sacred space within ourselves.

Meditation is a practice of stilling the mind and connecting with our inner being. It can be as simple as focusing on the breath or repeating a mantra. Prayer is another form of connecting with the divine and expressing gratitude. Whether it's a traditional prayer or simply speaking from the heart, prayer can bring us a sense of peace and comfort.

Chanting is a practice of using sound and vibration to connect with the divine. It can be a mantra, a chant from a specific tradition, or simply singing. Chanting can also have a powerful effect on our physical and emotional well-being.

Energy healing is the practice of balancing and restoring our energy field. It can be done through practices such as Reiki, acupuncture, or yoga. By working with the subtle energies of our body, we can promote healing and a deeper sense of connection with the sacred.

Incorporating these sacred rituals into our daily practice can bring us a sense of peace, grounding, and a deeper connection with the divine. It can be helpful to set aside a specific time each day to practice these rituals or to simply incorporate them into our daily routine whenever possible. By doing so, we can create a sacred space within ourselves and deepen our spiritual connection.

Opening and Balancing the Chakras through Meditation

The chakras are part of a system that is believed to affect the physical, emotional, and spiritual well-being of the user. When these chakras are blocked or unbalanced, we may experience physical or emotional discomfort, stress, or illness.

One powerful way to open and balance the chakras is through meditation. Meditation is the practice of focusing the mind on a particular object or thought to achieve a calm and peaceful state of being. It has been shown to reduce stress, improve emotional well-being, and enhance spiritual connection.

To begin a chakra meditation practice, find a quiet and comfortable space where you won't be interrupted. Sit or lie down in a comfortable position and take a few deep breaths to relax your body and calm your mind.

Begin by visualizing each of the seven chakras, starting from the root chakra at the base of the spine and moving up to the crown chakra at the top of the head. As you visualize each chakra, focus on its corresponding color and imagine a bright light flowing through it.

Next, focus on each chakra individually, beginning with the root chakra and moving up. As you focus on each chakra, repeat a specific affirmation or mantra that corresponds with that chakra. For example, the affirmation for the root chakra might be "I am safe and secure" or "I trust in my own power."

Continue this practice for as long as you like, taking deep breaths and allowing the energy to flow through each chakra. With consistent practice, you may find that you feel more grounded, centered, and balanced in your daily life.

Incorporating chakra meditation into your spiritual practice can deepen your connection to the sacred and help you achieve a greater sense of inner peace and well-being.

Incorporating Chakra Healing into Your Spiritual Practice

Chakra healing is a powerful tool for deepening your spiritual connection and bringing balance to your life. By working with the energy centers of the body, known as chakras, you can address physical, emotional, and spiritual imbalances and create a greater sense of harmony and well-being.

One way to incorporate chakra healing into your spiritual practice is through meditation. Meditation is a powerful tool for opening and balancing the chakras, and there are many different meditation techniques you can use to support this process. For example, you may choose to focus on a particular chakra while meditating, visualizing it as a glowing ball of light and feeling its energy flowing freely through your body.

Another way to work with the chakras is through energy healing practices such as Reiki or acupuncture. These modalities work with the body's subtle energy systems to help remove blockages and restore balance. By receiving regular energy healing sessions, you can support your chakras in staying open and balanced and deepen your overall spiritual practice.

Chakra chanting is another powerful way to incorporate chakra healing into your spiritual practice. By chanting the corresponding seed sounds for each chakra, you can activate and balance the energy centers in your body. This practice can also be combined with meditation, allowing you to focus on the vibration and energy of each chakra as you chant.

Finally, you may want to explore chakra sound healing, which uses the vibrational power of sound to balance and heal the chakras. This can be done through listening to specific chakra frequencies, or by using sound healing instruments like singing bowls or tuning forks.

Incorporating chakra healing into your spiritual practice can be a transformative experience. By working with the energy centers of the body, you can connect more deeply with the sacred within yourself and the world around you, and experience greater levels of balance, harmony, and spiritual growth.

Connecting with the Sacred through Chakra Work

Chakras are not only physical points in our body, but they also represent spiritual energy centers. Working on our chakras allows us to connect with the spiritual realm and deepen our connection with the sacred.

When we meditate on our chakras, we bring awareness to the energy flow in our body, and we allow the blockages to dissolve. The opening and balancing of our chakras bring us into a state of harmony, where we can access a deeper sense of connection with the divine.

Working with our chakras helps us to recognize the energy that flows through us and that is present in the world around us. This heightened awareness enables us to connect with the sacred in a deeper way. It allows us to recognize that everything is interconnected and that there is a profound energy that permeates the universe.

By paying attention to our chakras, we become more attuned to the spiritual energies that surround us. We can tune into the subtle frequencies and connect with the divine presence. This practice helps us to access the wisdom and guidance of the universe and bring it into our lives.

Incorporating chakra work into our spiritual practice allows us to connect with the sacred in a profound way. It brings us closer to the divine and helps us to recognize the interconnectedness of all things. This deepening of our spiritual connection can bring us a greater sense of purpose and meaning in our lives.

Chakra Chanting

Chanting is a powerful tool for opening and balancing the chakras. Each chakra is associated with a specific sound or vibration, and chanting these sounds can help to stimulate and balance the energy centers in your body.

To start, find a comfortable seated position and take a few deep breaths. Then, begin chanting the sound associated with the first chakra, which is "LAM". Repeat this sound several times, focusing your attention on the area at the base of your spine. Visualize a red, glowing ball of energy there, and feel it growing stronger and brighter with each repetition of the chant.

Move on to the second chakra, which is associated with the sound "VAM". Located just below the navel, this chakra is linked to the color orange. As you chant the sound, visualize a bright orange ball of energy in this area, and feel it becoming more vibrant and powerful.

Continue chanting through each of the chakras, focusing your attention on the corresponding area of the body and visualizing the associated color and energy. The sounds associated with each chakra are: "RAM" for the third chakra (solar plexus), "YAM" for the fourth chakra (heart), "HAM" for the fifth chakra (throat), "OM" for the sixth chakra (third eye), and "NG" for the seventh chakra (crown).

Chanting is a simple but powerful practice that can be incorporated into your daily spiritual routine. Experiment with different chants and mantras to find what resonates with you, and remember to focus on your breath and the physical sensations in your body as you chant. This practice can help to deepen your connection to the sacred and to bring more balance and harmony into your life.

Chakra Energy Healing

Chakra energy healing is a holistic practice that involves restoring the balance of the chakras and promoting physical, emotional, and spiritual well-being. It is a powerful way to enhance your spiritual practice and deepen your connection to the sacred.

Chakra energy healing is based on the idea that the chakras are centers of energy located along the spine that correspond to different aspects of the body, mind, and spirit. Each chakra is associated with a different color, symbol, and element and represents different aspects of our being.

When the chakras are blocked, stagnant, or out of balance, we may experience physical and emotional symptoms such as fatigue, anxiety, depression, pain, and illness. Chakra energy healing works by removing blockages and restoring the flow of energy, allowing for greater vitality, clarity, and peace.

There are different techniques used in chakra energy healing, including:

1. Reiki: This is a Japanese healing technique that uses the practitioner's hands to channel healing energy into the body to balance the chakras and promote relaxation and well-being.

2. Acupuncture: This is a traditional Chinese medicine technique that involves inserting fine needles into specific points along the meridians to unblock energy and promote healing.

3. Reflexology: This is a type of massage that focuses on applying pressure to specific points on the feet and hands that correspond to different organs and systems in the body, including the chakras.

4. Crystal healing: This involves using different types of crystals and gemstones to balance and harmonize the chakras, promoting healing and well-being.

No matter which technique you choose, chakra energy healing can be a powerful way to connect with the sacred and enhance your spiritual practice. By working to balance the chakras, you can promote physical, emotional, and spiritual health and deepen your connection to the divine.

Chakra Sound Healing

Chakra sound healing is a powerful way to balance and open your chakras. Sound has been used for centuries to heal the mind, body, and spirit, and it is an effective way to bring your chakras into balance.

Each chakra has a specific frequency and sound that corresponds to it, and when these sounds are played, they help to release any blockages that may be present in the chakra. Chakra sound healing can be done using a variety of instruments, including singing bowls, tuning forks, and even the human voice.

One of the most popular instruments used in chakra sound healing is the singing bowl. These bowls are made of different materials, such as crystal or metal, and they are played by striking or rubbing them with a mallet. Each bowl corresponds to a specific chakra, and when played, the vibrations help to balance and open that chakra.

Tuning forks are another tool used in chakra sound healing. They are designed to produce a specific frequency that corresponds to a particular chakra. When the fork is struck and placed on the body, the vibrations help to release any blockages in that chakra and bring it into balance.

The human voice can also be used in chakra sound healing. Chanting or toning the specific sound that corresponds to a particular chakra can help to balance and open that chakra. For example, chanting "om" for the crown chakra can help to release any blockages and bring it into balance.

Incorporating chakra sound healing into your spiritual practice can be a powerful way to deepen your connection with the sacred. By working with the specific frequencies and sounds that correspond to each chakra, you can release any blockages and bring your chakras into balance. This, in turn, can help to promote overall health and well-being in your mind, body, and spirit.

Chapter 15: Chakras and the Path of Enlightenment

The chakras are ancient spiritual energy centers that are believed to be responsible for our physical, emotional, and spiritual well-being. They are believed to be the gateway to higher consciousness and a pathway to enlightenment. In this final chapter, we'll explore the concept of chakras and how they can be used to support us on our journey toward greater awareness and understanding. We'll discuss how the chakras can help us to open up to more profound experiences and how we can use them to deepen our connection with the divine.

Understanding the Path of Enlightenment

Enlightenment, or the attainment of higher consciousness, has been a topic of discussion for centuries. It is often associated with the Eastern philosophy of spirituality, but in recent times, the quest for enlightenment has become a universal pursuit.

Enlightenment is not just a spiritual concept; it is a way of living. It is a state of being in which individual experiences a sense of oneness with the universe, and their life becomes a reflection of their inner harmony.

The path to enlightenment involves a profound shift in our perspective of the world around us. It requires us to look beyond the material world and to embrace our spiritual nature. Enlightenment is not easy, but it is worth it.

Enlightenment is not a destination; it is a continuous process of self-discovery. It involves a gradual expansion of consciousness and an awakening to the true nature of reality. This process can take years, if not decades, of committed spiritual practice, but the rewards are immeasurable.

In the final chapter of our book on Chakras, we explore the role of chakras in the journey to higher consciousness. Chakras are energy centers within our body that are connected to our physical, emotional, and spiritual well-being. By understanding and balancing our chakras, we can tap into the infinite wisdom and guidance of the universe, which can help us on our journey to enlightenment.

The Role of Chakras in the Journey to Higher Consciousness

The concept of chakras is rooted in ancient Hindu and Buddhist traditions, where they are considered as energy centers within the body that help regulate physical, emotional, and spiritual well-being. Chakras are believed to be connected to various bodily functions and have specific properties that affect a person's consciousness.

Chakras play a crucial role in the journey to higher consciousness. They are often considered as a gateway to accessing deeper levels of consciousness and spiritual growth. Each chakra governs specific physical and emotional areas, and their activation or blockage can have a significant impact on a person's overall well-being.

The process of balancing and activating chakras involves identifying any imbalances in the body's energy centers and taking steps to realign them. There are many ways to activate chakras, including meditation, yoga, visualization, and breathing techniques.

Meditation is particularly useful in activating and balancing chakras. Through meditation, one can access the deeper levels of consciousness and tap into the chakras' potential. Practicing mindful breathing can also help clear blockages and activate the energy centers.

Chakras can also be used as a tool for self-discovery and personal growth. As you begin to understand each chakra's significance and how they affect your body and mind, you can take steps to align them, resulting in a more balanced and healthier lifestyle.

Balancing and Activating Chakras

The key to unlocking the power of the chakras lies in finding balance and activating them to their fullest potential. Each chakra represents a different aspect of our being, and it is essential to balance them all to achieve optimal health and well-being.

To begin balancing your chakras, begin with the root chakra and work your way up. Root chakras are located at the base of the spine and represent our connection to the physical world. This chakra can be balanced through grounding practices such as yoga, walking barefoot on the earth, and eating root vegetables.

Moving up the body, the sacral chakra is located just below the navel and represents our creativity and emotional well-being. This chakra can be balanced through creative activities, such as art or dance, and by honoring our emotions through journaling or therapy.

The solar plexus chakra is in the upper abdomen and represents our personal power and self-esteem. This chakra can be balanced through activities that promote confidence and self-love, such as affirmations or practicing self-care.

The heart chakra, located at the center of the chest, represents love and compassion. Balancing this chakra can be achieved through acts of kindness, volunteering, or practicing forgiveness and letting go of grudges.

Moving higher up the body, the throat chakra represents communication and self-expression. Balancing this chakra can be done through speaking your truth, singing, or practicing active listening.

The third eye chakra, located between the eyebrows, represents intuition and inner wisdom. Balancing this chakra can be done through meditation, journaling, or practicing mindfulness.

Finally, the crown chakra, located at the top of the head, represents our connection to the divine. Balancing this chakra can be achieved through spiritual practices such as prayer, meditation, or spending time in nature.

In addition to balancing the chakras, it is essential to activate them to their fullest potential. This can be done through practices such as visualization, sound healing, and working with crystals that correspond to each chakra.

Balancing and activating the chakras takes time and practice, but the benefits of achieving a harmonious and balanced system are immeasurable. Take the time to explore these practices and unlock the full potential of your chakras on your journey to higher consciousness.

Importance of Meditation in the Journey

Meditation is a powerful tool that can help us on our journey to higher consciousness. Practicing meditation gives us the chance to not only release our own pent-up emotions but to quiet our minds and strengthen our self-awareness. This connection allows us to tap into our intuition and access deeper levels of awareness.

Meditation can also help us balance and activate our chakras. When we meditate, we focus our attention on our breath and the present moment. This focus can help us become more aware of the energy flowing through our chakras and identify any imbalances or blockages.

In addition to balancing and activating our chakras, meditation can also help us release negative emotions and thoughts that may be holding us back. As we meditate, we can observe these thoughts and emotions without judgment and learn to let them go.

It's important to note that meditation is a practice that requires patience and dedication. It's not something that we can master overnight, and we may encounter challenges along the way. However, by consistently practicing meditation and incorporating it into our daily routine, we can reap the many benefits that it offers on our journey to higher consciousness.

Overcoming Challenges in the Journey to Higher Consciousness

As with any journey, the path to higher consciousness and enlightenment is not without its challenges. These challenges can manifest in many forms and may vary from person to person. However, certain challenges are common to most people on this path, and it's important to understand them and find ways to overcome them.

One of the biggest challenges is the resistance of the ego. The ego is a construct of the mind that is designed to keep us safe and comfortable. It creates a sense of identity and separateness, which can be difficult to let go of when we are striving for higher consciousness. The ego can cause us to doubt ourselves, become defensive, and resist change.

Another common challenge is the fear of the unknown. As we move along the path to higher consciousness, we may encounter experiences and realities that are unfamiliar to us. This can be scary and can cause us to question whether we are on the right path or not. There may be times when we feel overwhelmed and uncertain about the future. One of the ways to overcome these challenges is through self-awareness and mindfulness. By observing our thoughts and emotions without judgment, we can become more aware of how our ego is holding us back. We can begin to question the validity of our thoughts and beliefs and start to see through the illusions created by the ego.

It's also important to develop a regular meditation practice. Meditation helps to quiet the mind and connect us with our higher self. Through regular meditation, we can develop greater clarity and insight into our true nature, which can help to dissolve the resistance of the ego and overcome the fear of the unknown.

Finally, it's important to stay connected with a community of like-minded individuals who are also on the path to higher consciousness. Surrounding ourselves with supportive and uplifting people can provide us with the encouragement and motivation we need to keep going when the journey becomes challenging.

Please Leave a Review!

If you've enjoyed this book, please leave a review on the retailer's website where you obtained your copy from. It will be highly appreciated and helps me out a lot! Thanks again.

Don't miss out!

Visit the website below and you can sign up to receive emails whenever Maya Whitaker publishes a new book. There's no charge and no obligation.

https://books2read.com/r/B-A-RVFZ-NZBLC

BOOKS 2 READ

Connecting independent readers to independent writers.